National Curriculum requirements and the growing awareness of the relevance of popular culture to children's experience have meant that media education is now firmly established as a part of the primary curriculum.

Media Education in the Primary School provides a clear, practical guide for teachers on how to approach media education. The book offers helpful ways into areas such as teaching about media institutions, news and the concept of representation, as well as more easily accessible topics such as soaps, comics and advertising. Cross-curricular classroom activities such as video work, simulating advertising campaigns, photography and storyboarding are also included. All the activities have been thoroughly tested, and are fully compatible with current National Curriculum requirements.

Carol Craggs sets the activities firmly within a theoretical framework. She clarifies key issues and identifies appropriate teaching methods, putting the emphasis on active child-centred learning and a collaborative approach. In addition, she provides an appendix of National Curriculum requirements for easy reference to simplify record-keeping and assessment.

Media Education in the Primary School is an essential guide for primary and middle school teachers, especially those approaching media education for the first time. It will also provide an informative introduction to the subject for all students and teachers of education.

Carol Craggs has been a full-time teacher for twenty years and is English Co-ordinator at a school in Nottinghamshire.

Media Education in the Primary School

Carol E. Craggs

London and New York

First published 1992
by Routledge
11 New Fetter Lane, London EC4P 4EE

Simultaneously published in the USA and Canada
by Routledge
a division of Routledge, Chapman and Hall, Inc.
29 West 35th Street, New York, NY 10001

Typeset in 10 on 12 Palatino by
Florencetype Limited, Kewstoke, Avon
Printed in Great Britain by
T J Press (Padstow) Ltd, Padstow, Cornwall

British Library Cataloguing in Publication Data
A catalogue record for this book is available from the British Library.

Library of Congress Cataloging in Publication Data
Craggs, Carol E. (Carol Elizabeth)
    Media education in the primary school / by Carol E. Craggs.
      p.   cm.
    Includes bibliographical references (p.).
      1. Mass media—study and teaching (Elementary)   I. Title.
P91.3.C69   1992
372.83—dc20   91-40383

ISBN 0-415-06370-1
      0-415-06371-X (pbk)

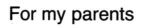
For my parents

Contents

Acknowledgements

Although the actual compiling of this book took a mere eighteen months, nevertheless it is the result of many hundreds of hours spent in the primary classroom experimenting with, and adapting, ideas – both my own and those of others. Consequently I would like to thank everyone who has supported and encouraged me over the past six years.

My greatest debt must go to Dr Len Masterman, without whose inspiration the book would never have been written. His belief in my ability as a classroom teacher has enabled me to achieve more than I could have imagined.

Secondly I would like to thank all of the children at Stevenson School in Stapleford who have shown such enormous enthusiasm for media education. Their responses have proved how exciting this area of the curriculum can be. These young people have taught me a great deal, especially that we should not underestimate the primary child's ability to consider sophisticated social issues. I especially wish to thank the children whose words are quoted in the text.

Next I must thank my professional colleagues with whom I have worked. Special thanks are due to: Ann Binger, Dave Chapple, Terry Maxwell, Stuart McFarlane, Toni Shepherd, Margaret Smith and Pat Wearn who not only have tolerated my evangelism for media education but most of whom have become converts.

As the anecdotal nature of the book demonstrates, most of my classroom research has been carried out whilst teaching full time, but I would like to express a deep gratitude to Nottinghamshire County Council, which funded my secondment to read for an MPhil degree at the University of

Nottingham. It was a great privilege to have a year to work alongside colleagues, share practice and reflect on what is really important in the primary curriculum.

There are so many people to thank personally but Barry Ecuyer, the talented artist and experienced primary school media teacher who has created the pictures which precede each of the practical chapters, deserves a special mention. Barry gave me these drawings when I was having self-doubts. I would also like to thank Dr John Bastiani, Sue Archbold, Jan Stewart, Rosemary Fraser and Terry Dolan, who helped me in different ways whilst I was at university.

Thanks must also go to Van den Berghs for their kind permission to use the advertisement for Stork margarine. I am most grateful, too, to Lever Brothers Limited for their permission to reproduce the Persil promotion leaflet.

I would like to record my thanks to the members of Nottinghamshire Media Education, a group of dedicated teachers with whom I have had the good fortune to work. Special thanks are due to: Sue Butterworth, Pat Gray, Mike Hamlin, Paul Kiddey and Pete Roberts.

Last, but not least, I need to thank my husband Matthew for his criticism and help at every stage of the creation of this book.

Introduction

True literacy in our time encompasses media education.[1]

With the introduction of the National Curriculum, media education should soon be an established feature of primary classroom practice. The document *English for ages 5–16*[2] contains a separate section devoted to media education and, more importantly, it is an integral theme in the Programmes of Study. It is now recognised that books are just one medium of communication and we must accept that the young people who sit in our classrooms will, in the future, be gleaning even more of their everyday information from television, newspapers, radio, films, computers and other technological media. The children need to learn how to make sense of this invasion of information in order to take charge of their own lives and to enhance the pleasure they receive from the media. Already there is a growing number of primary teachers who recognise the importance of encouraging pupils to study the media in order that they may analyse the inevitably selective and constructed nature of media messages and examine the possible influence these may have in shaping our perceptions of reality. To be effective in integrating this learning into the curriculum we need to broaden our understanding of the term literacy so as to embrace the specific skill of media literacy.

The average primary school teacher is highly skilled at accommodating new curriculum areas and coping with the changing needs of the children, but it would be fair to say that media education is still relatively underdeveloped in this sector. The National Curriculum may be advocating the critical reading of media texts and as teachers we may be anxious to include the children's popular culture in our curricula, but how is this to be achieved, what resources are available, which Attainment Targets can be reached through this work, how may colleagues and parents react to children reading comics in class or discussing a video tape of soap opera title sequences and how can we engage the parents' active involvement? These are some of the issues which will be addressed by this book, which is essentially a practical handbook of activities and teaching strategies that I have found to be effective in my own classroom. Nevertheless, media education is underpinned by sound theoretical principles and so, in addition to the material contained in the next chapter, throughout the text there is an attempt to blend a soupçon of this theory with the practical ingredients. This will ensure that the activities are approached within a considered conceptual framework which should be conducive to continuity and development.

THE ARGUMENTS FOR PRIMARY MEDIA EDUCATION

The first task though is to clarify the rationale for media education at the primary level. Government endorsements, however welcome, are no replacements for carefully reasoned educational arguments.

Media consumption

It has been estimated that the average school child sees television for about twenty hours each week[3] and most children have access to newspapers, videos, computer programs, radio, magazines and comics. The mass media are undeniably important parts of everyone's cultural environment and, if for no other reason, this fact alone should convince primary teachers to include media education in the curriculum, but it is not simply the volume of media saturation which is significant. Almost certainly these ubiquitous social influences have a qualitative role to play in the child's understanding of the world. For example, soap operas, situation comedies, game shows, and so on, often contribute to the perpetuation of traditional gender roles and to the child's sense of identity. Furthermore, in these genres, ethnic minorities, older members of the community and the disabled are frequently represented as stereotypes which reinforce social misconceptions. In schools we cannot afford to ignore these powerful influences; instead we need to encourage children to deconstruct texts so that they can begin to question both the manifest and covert values which are transmitted by the mass media. Like many other basic life skills this process should be developed in the primary school.

The evolution of literacy

The government's laudable aim is to devise a 'school curriculum which will develop the potential of all pupils and equip them for the challenges of employment in tomorrow's world'.[4] Few would contest the argument that literacy is a fundamental curriculum concern, but how is literacy to be defined? Preconceived assumptions of what it entails need to be revised in the light of what 'tomorrow's world' may demand of citizens.

In the coming decades media consumption is predicted to increase and many future social and educational changes are likely to arise from technological advances in the communication networks. The cosy notion, expressed by some critics, of reclaiming the basics – those mythical standards of a bygone era – is more than dubious. Obviously children must be taught to read print effectively and strategies should be developed to advance this crucial skill, but what was basic literacy two decades ago is not compatible with current needs. Instead of 'going back to basics' – that Gradgrindian utilitarianism which is meaningless in the knowledge of today's flow of information – we need to protect the future needs of young children by providing a curriculum where basic literacy is more than a marketable ability to read and write and where it extends to the interpretation of texts born of technology and commercialism. This implies that we must go 'forward to basics'.[5] The sooner we can encourage our students to reject the idea that the media are 'windows on the world' and then enable them to penetrate television's representation of reality to identify its processes of production, the sooner we shall produce citizens who can, where and when necessary, read against the media's manufactured representations.

Education for citizenship

If we are serious in wishing to equip children for the 'responsibilities of citizenship' then education for democracy cannot afford to be left to chance. When they are adults our pupils will rely heavily on the media for information and 'control over the means of informing people is the basis of political power'.[6] Already research indicates that the media, especially television, are believed to be important factors in determining how people exercise their democratic rights,[7] and the meticulous care with which television divides air time among the various political parties during elections is witness to this influence. No candidate must be seen to be given an unfair advantage.

To direct children's natural curiosity to enquire how the media select their images and construct narratives and to encourage them to question media representations can be an enfranchising experience. If our culturally inherent sexism and racism, which often operate at a semantic level,[8] are transmitted as the norm by media representations, they may not be seen to exist and so they cannot be challenged. The general acceptance of established cultural norms by the media removes, to some extent, the children's freedom to resist accepting them, for only when they are aware that alternatives are available can they begin to confront what is taken for granted and see it with fresh eyes. If primary education seeks to improve rather than reproduce society, then media education has the power to provide children with the skills and confidence to make their own judgements without fear or favour.

It has been suggested that primary education is 'an invitation to consider what qualities will be valued in an uncertain future' and that we are 'to try in so far as we are able to make our children's education future proof'.[9] If this is accepted, then an ability to analyse media evidence must contribute towards the democratic health of the nation. Moreover, the pedagogy which is most conducive to media education is non-authoritarian, action-orientated, process-based and cooperative and one in which the atmosphere allows decisions to be taken regularly, on a democratic basis.

Child-centred learning

A fundamental intention of the primary school is to foster an intrinsic love of learning. Although the phrase 'child-centred education' is terminology which was fashionable in the 1960s and 1970s, most teachers would agree that worthwhile learning which arises from the child's experiences and environment is desirable, and obviously motivation is improved if teaching is harnessed to what is meaningful and pleasurable. No curriculum which is remote from these factors would be successful at primary level. To introduce popular culture into the classroom in a non-judgemental way both captivates the children's attention and enhances a belief in their own values and self-worth, especially if the teacher shows that she too shares their pleasure.

It could be argued that teachers working in this sector have always used the media, perhaps as stimuli to teach about other things, but this is not media education. A reversal of direction, which focuses on the processes of mediation rather than on its contents, is now required. Media education is essentially a critical practice and must not be relegated to a servicing role. However, it must be pointed out that a host of the National Curriculum's Attainment Targets – in various subject areas – can be successfully achieved incidentally via media education. Whilst some teachers, quite rightly, may be uneasy about the content of some television programmes, newspapers, pop videos and so on, media education is neither an inoculation against the media nor an acceptance of its values, rather it is a celebratory experience which intends to direct the children's critical faculties and natural curiosity to question what they thought they already knew.

Investigating and reflecting

After nurturing the desire to learn comes the basic need to help children learn how to learn and this task engages the efforts of primary teachers for a large proportion of every working day. 'Merely to absorb facts is of only of slight value in the present, and usually of even less value in the future. Learning how to learn is the element that is always of value now and in the future'.[10] Media education generally is not concerned with the presentation of information; rather it is the shared exploration of how meanings are encoded and decoded. It is concerned with teaching children to think for themselves and it requires teachers to reject the notion of what Paulo Freire described as the 'banking' system of education. This system regards children as if they were containers to be filled with knowledge by the teacher.

The more completely he fills the receptacles, the better teacher he is. The more meekly the receptacles permit themselves to be filled the better students they are. [He goes on to argue that] Only dialogue, which requires critical thinking, is also capable of generating critical thinking. Without dialogue there can be no communication and without communication there can be no true education.[11]

Freire advocates that the relationship between the pupil and the teacher should be one of mutual respect, one in which the learner's experience is valued so that a dialogue, which is a genuine exchange of knowledge, can exist.

Media education lends itself to this kind of dialogue because even young children have experienced thousands of hours of exposure to media products. Such a dialogue demands confidence; the teacher has to accept that she does not know all of the answers but that she needs to gain new understandings alongside the children. Moreover, once the dialogue is opened the teacher has to resist making judgements and imposing her values on the pupils. This kind of atmosphere is a vital requirement for media education, as pedagogy itself transmits messages which are all the more potent for their being tacit. Although this issue is explored in more detail in the next chapter it needs to be said here that if the pedagogy is authoritarian and elitist, if the teacher knows all of the answers, then it is virtually impossible for the children to achieve rational, democratic decisions. What is more, an authoritarian pedagogy would subdue the questioning attitude that media education is seeking to engender.

The majority of primary school children are at Piaget's stage of concrete operations in their cognitive development and much of their learning depends on practical experience which will advance their growth towards rational thinking and the final stage of formal operations. Therefore the process of discovery permeates most areas of classroom learning. It is one of the intentions of media education to develop in children the means of discovering how to be critical for themselves so that they can become independent from the teacher. This ability is facilitated by discovering how the media operate, and the process of this learning relies on the children's active participation. It is sensible, therefore, to begin media education in the primary school, where structured discovery and open, investigative activities are the accepted methods of learning.

Cross-curricular teaching

Up to now I have argued that media education is highly compatible with the basic educational philosophy and pedagogy of the primary school, but there are also arguments which point to the fact that the organisation of the primary classroom is the most suitable for its implementation. Here the curriculum is not organised on subject-centred principles and even within the guidelines of the National Curriculum the government

> believe it to be important that schools should have flexibility about how they organise their teaching. The description of the national curriculum in terms of foundation subjects is not a description of how the school day should be organised and the curriculum delivered.[12]

Media education at this level does not have to jostle with other subjects for a place in the curriculum, as it might be required to do so later on, because, in the primary school, knowledge is usually regarded holistically. Therefore media can be taught across the curriculum in the same way as language or multicultural education. Timetables do not constrain continuity so pedagogy can be naturally exploratory rather than didactic and we have the ability to integrate and extend our subject matter in the knowledge of the needs of our individual classes. Viewed from this perspective media education can be seen as an inseparable and stimulating element within the existing curriculum and a valuable and inspiring extra dimension. Consequently no teacher need regard media as a threatening extra burden to be accommodated into an already overloaded timetable.

CODA

Finally it must be stressed that media education in the primary school is not to be confused with the types of courses in media studies that are implemented at GCSE level, even though the understanding gained in the earlier years will lay the foundations for these qualifications. Nor is media education a scion to be grafted onto the main branch of the primary school curriculum, for its incipient life force is present in the roots of what is already accepted. What is necessary is that we make way for its growth by clarifying the key issues, building a conceptual framework and developing practical approaches, so that its blossoms can enrich and strengthen a curriculum whose content intends 'to develop in pupils those personal qualities which cannot be written into any programme of study or attainment target'.[13]

Chapter 1

Starting points

The actual learning depends on children experiencing the consequences of their own action rather than those of the teacher's instruction.[1]

Even though the reader may accept the rationale for primary schools developing media education, arguments alone are inadequate. We need to be aware of precisely what is entailed, what mistakes need to be avoided, which approaches are the most effective in the classroom and what kind of pedagogy is compatible with the philosophy of the subject area. In my experience of in-service work with teachers, in the wake of the initial requests for suggestions for classroom activities usually comes an interest in knowing something of the theoretical principles and historical background to media education. There is a need to see practice in the light of theory and theory in the light of practice. Therefore this chapter intends, firstly, to furnish the reader with a brief overview of the literature and research findings, secondly, to clarify the major underlying key issues for primary school media education today and, thirdly, to identify the criteria which contribute to a conducive pedagogy. All three issues need to be on the agenda for examination and discussion if we are to promote the evolution of sound classroom practice.

AN OUTLINE HISTORY: FROM DISCRIMINATION TO DEMYTHOLOGISING

Literature specifically advocating or describing primary school media education has, up until very recently, been scarce, but it has been produced in relation to the secondary curriculum since the 1930s. It is worth knowing just a little about the evolution of

these educational approaches so that the pitfalls and misunder-
standings of the past can be rejected.

1930–1970: popular culture versus school values

Half a century ago any official educational reference to the
media was always disparaging and the influence of popular
culture was only grudgingly acknowledged when it could no
longer be ignored. This influence was regarded as 'subtly cor-
rupting the taste and habit of a rising generation'[2] and the
directive to the teacher was to inoculate the pupils against its
depravity. This message was echoed in 1959 in the Crowther
Report[3] when the teacher was urged to treat the media 'with the
discrimination that only education can give'.

An earlier embodiment of this thinking was proposed in
1933 by the Cambridge academics F. R. Leavis and D.
Thompson in the book *Culture and Environment*,[4] which was to
influence the teaching of English for the next three decades.
This book was a battlecry for established literary culture to be
used as a sword to humiliate and suppress the popular cultural
values transmitted by the media in the interests of 'maintaining continuity' of traditional standards, and teachers were
recommended to label the media with a caveat. It could not be
envisaged that popular and traditional literary tastes could
coexist without value judgements and comparisons. Rather the
pupil was to 'be trained to discriminate and resist' the mass
media which offered 'satisfaction at the lowest level'.[5]
Fundamentally it was this mode of thinking that prevailed in
educational establishments until the early 1960s, although it
was now acknowledged that media influences had educational
implications.

The academic, if not the official, tide was beginning to turn
with publications such as Richard Hoggart's *The Uses of Literacy*
in 1957,[6] and in 1964 Hall and Whannel's *The Popular Arts*[7]
helped to wash away some of the contempt for the culture of the
mass media. The prevailing attitude was now becoming, not
total resistance, but discrimination, and this attitude was dis-
cernible in the *Newsom Report* of 1963,[8] which strongly advocated the study of film and television. The report, however,
asserted that the values of the media were often at variance with
those of the schools and suggested that 'we need to train children to look critically and discriminate what is good and bad in

what they see' (§475). In this document there were undoubtedly signs of progress in the development of attitudes to media studies but the criteria were still firmly rooted in established literary values. These evaluative criteria hung on the subject like second-hand cumbersome and ill-fitting garments and so media education stagnated in spite of an urgent need for a more positive and realistic approach. In addition it was likely that there was some reticence amongst teachers to acknowledge that the popular tastes of children could have any value in the school curriculum.

1970–1990: a change of heart

There were few positive official responses in the following decade and the next constructive advice came in 1975 in the *Bullock Report*.[9] It applauded the 'serious study of the medium of television' but despite such enlightened proclamations there was still the vestigial presence of the earlier discriminatory approach. From the 1980s onwards publications advocating media studies in the secondary sector were beginning to emanate from insightful educators and academics,[10] but nothing more hopeful was published from official sources until 1983 when the Department of Education and Science produced the report *Popular TV and Schoolchildren*.[11] This document was refreshing in that it sought to clarify and describe attitudes and representations and, although it collected data on viewing patterns, it made no pretence at having produced empirical evidence of television's effects. Although the tone of the report was occasionally judgemental, its final pronouncement was that 'Schools . . . must review their responsibilities with reference to young people's experience of television . . . specialist courses in media studies are not enough: all teachers should be involved in examining and discussing television programmes with young people'.

Before proceeding to consider the requirements of the National Curriculum, I feel that, although this is merely an overview of the history of media education, something must be said about the immense influence of Roland Barthes – the French semiologist and philosopher of culture, whose essays *Mythologies* were first published in 1957.[12] (An English translation was not available until 1972.) Barthes' writing is trenchant and radical. The essays were first published in popular magazines and they accorded equal importance to a wide variety of cultural artefacts. He describes wrestling, soap powder advertisements, cookery advice in magazines, the Citroen car and so on in ways which invite us to reconsider their cultural significance. Each essay is an attempt to account in detail for how petit bourgeois culture is transformed into a universal nature. However, it is in the last essay – 'Myth Today' – that Barthes explains that it is language itself which mystifies our perception and cloaks it in what he terms 'myth'. Although this essay is by no means easy to understand, it is of great importance to all media teachers, because it explains how myth represses politics and changes history into nature. As Barthes said in the preface to *Mythologies*, history and nature are 'confused at every turn . . . in the decorative display of what-goes-without-saying' and he wanted to 'explain these examples of the falsely obvious'. He considers that language, which is the expression of our culture, has already parcelled up meaning for us and he argues that it is our taken-for-granted acceptance of everyday culture which often blinds us to our real political and social position. Barthes wrote his *Mythologies* before the era of television as we know it, but when we reflect on how the smooth flow of this medium denies the complex selection processes which are involved in the manufacturing of its images, it is clear how television speaks in the language of myth. Media literacy requires us to rip away the taken-for-granted, to describe afresh what we see in the media and then analyse, confront, question and challenge it if necessary. The relevance of Barthes' work cannot be dismissed as academic – it illuminated the way ahead.

The document *English for ages 5–16* of the National Curriculum[13] adopts the most enlightened approach to media education of any official document. The authors 'considered media education largely as part of the exploration of popular culture, alongside more traditional literary texts' and accepted that it 'aims to develop systematically children's critical and creative powers through analysis and production of media artefacts'. Media education as described in this document is in the mode of demythologising not discriminating.

RESEARCH: HELP OR HINDRANCE?

There has been a plethora of empirical studies which attempt to chart the effects that the media have on young minds. Clearly they must have an effect on the way children relate to their environment but the media are influential only in conjunction with other socialising agencies, so, whilst teachers cannot ignore empirical evidence of effects, a trust in statistics perhaps ought to be tempered by a pragmatic scepticism. Most of the established research in this area tends to focus on the adversely imitative and aggressive effects,[14] and the results of these studies are necessarily inconclusive by virtue of the social impossibility of controlling the variables. It is this type of effects research which appears to have motivated the design, implementation and evaluation of many experimental media literacy courses in North America.[15] Mostly these courses are highly prescriptive; take no genuine account of the cognitive or social development of the children and generally fail to acknowledge that the viewer/reader is an active participant in the creation of meaning.

Although this does not mean that all of the material in these courses is unhelpful, it does indicate that we need to look elsewhere for more constructive advice. Australian educators have a tradition of primary media education and several comprehensive schemes of work have been produced which may be useful for readers who are new to media education.[16] Whilst it is beyond the scope of this chapter to discuss their research methodology at any great length, it is worth mentioning that the following notable Australian researchers, having rejected the 'effects' model, produced findings which are useful to those of us working in the classroom. Hodge and Tripp[17] took a semiotic approach to reveal how young people derive meaning from television. They found that although children interpreted television programmes in a highly complex way it was quite different from the manner in which adults interpreted them. In this respect their findings support the earlier studies of the psychologist Noble.[18] From this knowledge it follows that, as teachers, we must not presume, for example, that our interpretation of a cartoon resembles that of the child. Another Australian, Patricia Palmer, used symbolic interactionism to study children's consumption of television in a familial environment.[19] Like those of Hodge and Tripp, her data revealed that children participated actively whilst watching television and were not the slack-mouthed, glazed-eyed zombies which we have been warned that television creates. Rather she found that the medium is an important contributor to the learning process.

KEY ISSUES

It must be stated at the beginning that media education's subject matter is to a great extent ephemeral and dependent on the current interests, social needs and cognitive abilities of the pupils. Therefore the content must be negotiable and cannot be planned far in advance. The subject matter does not lend itself to right and wrong answers but rather seeks to enable young people to learn to question the processes which shape media messages. There is no need to build up fixed bodies of knowledge because the focus is directed towards the promotion of critical practices and intellectual functioning. Consequently prescriptive schemes of work may be unhelpful. However, this process-orientated approach is not an excuse for being vague; media education is too important to be left in a nebulous Utopia. Whilst accepting that there will always be room for debate and development, I would suggest that there are four key areas of investigation which underpin what is taught in media education at primary level. These are:

1. Selection and construction
2. A sense of audience
3. Representations of reality
4. Narrative techniques.

These are to be regarded not as mutually exclusive but rather as interrelated and reciprocating areas of concern which help govern practice. The quintessential needs are, firstly, to identify what understanding the children bring to their interpretation of media products and, secondly, to provide experiences which enhance their critical abilities.

Selection and construction

Establishing that what is seen on television, read in newspapers or heard on the radio is essentially selected and constructed by media professionals rather than a faithful, impartial representation of the truth is at the pinnacle in the hierarchy of media education's concerns. Deconstructing the economic, creative and technical processes through which media products pass en route to the consumer exposes the fact that decisions are unavoidably imbued with the ideologies and values of the creators. All too often the viewer's or reader's clarity of vision is blinkered by cultural and media conventions. We do not disagree with what is seen to be the norm because we perceive no conflict. For instance, we expect the managing director of a leading industry to be interviewed in a booklined study, whereas his striking labourers have to give their views on the situation against the roar of the traffic on the pavement outside the factory. The positioning of a microphone to pick up selected voices, the angle of the camera which gives prominence to chosen images, the juxtapositioning of particular television news items, and so on, are all conscious decisions which contribute to an overall viewpoint.

To question what determines the multitude of choices which are involved is the next logical step. Advertising often has an overriding influence on the selection of material for commercial television programmes and advertising revenue is an important factor in the viability of newspapers. A simple exploration of commercial and economic, political and legal influences on media decisions causes one to ask the questions: who controls the media and in whose interests are the selections made? As soon as these questions are posed, the apparent neutrality of mediation crumbles and inevitable partiality is seen as an integral component rather than as a sinister additive. Teaching about the notion of bias may be unhelpful if it presupposes the existence of impartiality, although it is important to recognise and distinguish between the integral partiality and that which is added as an extra and conscious ingredient.[20] If the concern of media neutrality is approached from how selectivity is built into media representations, children can explore for themselves how the dominant social values often innocently influence media choices and guide viewers and readers into accepting what are sometimes described as 'preferred meanings'.[21]

The very existence of a caption for a newspaper photograph frequently proves that the image is not self-sufficient in communicating the photographer's message, so exercises which strip words from pictures or which attempt to create commentary for ambiguous or 'neutral' images reveal that the 'text directs the reader through the signifieds of the image, causing him to avoid some and receive others'.[22] By analysing the way meaning enters an image and through exploring how these meanings are circulated and whose viewpoint they represent, the children can understand how any media text will inevitably be the product of value judgements. Therefore it is helpful if these texts are read actively in the knowledge of the editing techniques and conventions of the transmitting medium.

A sense of audience

To imagine that the messages encoded in media texts are imparted to an audience which simply and uniformly absorbs them is to ignore both the interaction of the communication processes and audience diversity. The notion that the same message can be received with a variety of results is as old as the Biblical parable of the sower and the seed.[23] Like all communication it is a two-way transaction: it consists of what the medium is representing to the child and how her experience actively operates on the material to make sense of it.

Stuart Hall[24] suggests that there are 'three hypothetical positions' from which to decode. The first of these is an unquestioning acceptance of the text, which he calls 'the dominant-hegemonic position' and this conveys the dominant values of society. Secondly he suggests that there is 'the negotiated position', which accepts as legitimate the basic established definitions but recognises that there are exceptions to the general rules. Thirdly he proposes that there is 'the oppositional code' in which the receiver 'detotalises the message in the preferred code in order to retotalise the message within some alternative framework of reference'. In this code the reader may interpret 'national interest' as 'class interest'. Hall is arguing that no television programme's meaning is entirely closed, but which of the codes the viewer adopts depends on her own framework of knowledge and the conditions of her existence.

Placing the child in the position of the media producer can enable her to understand how she is positioned as a viewer. Maybe she is being addressed as a member of a family, as a child, as a member of the white middle-class society, as an ethnic minority, as a female, and so on. Categorising an audience in this way makes it apparent that some social groups are rarely addressed by the media – groups such as the very old, the mentally disabled, members of certain religious or political persuasions, and so on. This realisation, together with an understanding of scheduling policy, will demonstrate that television's obsession with audience research and rating figures is ultimately concerned with economic factors rather than the viewers' intrinsic pleasures and opinions. If a video camera is available it is possible for upper junior pupils to create a television magazine programme for a group of infants or maybe for some elderly people they know. The children will need to consider: the attention span of their audience, their current interests, where and when they will be watching and with whom, whether advertising would support the programme, how the viewers may respond, and so on. Through using media technology children can develop their awareness of how a sense of audience is inscribed within the text and how the producers objectify their audience by presenting it with a very particular space to occupy.

Representations of reality

Because television selects its stories from virtually an infinite number of possibilities and furthermore constructs its representations to offer us an illusion of seamless reality, it is important that young viewers and readers are encouraged to explore the process of how media realism is produced. Authoritative documentaries and news broadcasts all involve selection and rely on a set of assumptions and values such as ethnocentrism, elitism, negativity, and so on. It is relatively simple to devise simulation exercises which help the children to understand how news is 'packaged' for the consumer. Once these processes have been opened out, the flow of realism has been interrupted and it becomes apparent that what masquerades as actuality is in fact a professionally presented viewpoint. Additionally, these types of learning activities can often reveal who has access to social power and consequently whose version of reality we are seeing.

It has been argued that the media influence whilst they appear merely to reflect and so they can be thought of as 'consciousness industries'.[25] Although no empirical evidence exists to support the notion, intuitively it would seem reasonable to expect that the accumulation of negative or positive stereotypical representations of social groups would influence the public's response to them. Stereotyping is not simply a way of categorising; it also implies a value judgement which viewers and readers are urged to endorse with unquestioning acceptance. Media representation is often largely determined by media construction. Consequently, if we simulate the processes through which the media manufacture their representations of women, ethnic groups, the class system, the elderly and so on, it may be possible to provide valuable, and sometimes unexpected, insights.

Distinguishing between reality and representations of reality, even in popular programmes such as soap operas, is frequently problematic. Viewers are encouraged to identify with the contemporary controversial issues which are embraced within the narrative and this reinforces the viewers' suspension of disbelief, but media realism is carefully contrived and works only because we accept the conventions. If we crack the rules of the convention we also crack the idea that the media are 'windows on the world'. They are presenting us not with reality but with a series of conventions which signify the real. It is hard to break with these dominant conventions but if children explore the codes which are employed by television and then experiment by breaking these rules it becomes easier to challenge the taken-for-granted.

Narrative techniques

Barthes said that narrative was 'simply there, like life itself',[26] so it is unremarkable that media material is largely organised and balanced according to a narrative structure. The story is the natural packaging for information and so the structure itself is taken for granted and is invisible. We forget that information has undergone the process of being moulded into an acceptable and entertaining story. Consequently it is possible, and enlightening, to analyse any media product in terms of the storyline, whether it is a news broadcast, a documentary film, a newspaper feature, an advertisement, a comic strip, a pop music video, or whatever. So that the children can appreciate how the imposition of this structure on the media's raw material shapes the finished product it is important that we enable them to explore the aesthetic processes of story making. For example, storyboards can be drawn for title sequences, picture stories can be created by taking a series of photographs, storylines may be teased from magazine advertisements and re-sequencing games using cut-up comic strips can be played. Once children sense the ubiquitous presence of narrative they also become aware of the need for a repertoire of characters, locations and plots all of which have been chosen and created to construct perspectives for the media consumer.

Footnote to the key issues

I have purposefully made no concession for the primary school in defining what I believe are the underlying key issues for media education, as from my experience I know it is possible to approach these issues in some honest and enjoyable form at this level. Obviously they can be achieved only by devising learning situations which match the children's cognitive abilities and the pupils must express the understandings which they gain in their own language. If we are seeking for a psychological framework for this approach to learning it would be that of J.S. Bruner.[27]

Bruner's educational theory modified and extended the Piagetian theory of learning. He believed that 'knowing' develops through the interaction of the individual with the environment and that it is, for the most part, heuristic learning. Because the world is highly complex he argues that children employ strategies to reduce that complexity so that they can comprehend it. He proposed that it is the fundamental principles that give structure to curriculum content and that 'concepts should be developed and re-developed in a "spiralling" sequence towards greater levels of abstraction'.[28] This caused him to propose that any subject 'may be taught to anybody at any age in some form'. As far as primary science is concerned this is now an accepted approach. The National Curriculum science document demands that we offer an introduction to physical scientific concepts such as that of sinking and floating (A T 10 level 3),[29] although we are not expected to finalise the learning in this area at Key Stage 2. Consequently we should not be afraid to introduce children to practical work which may eventually help them to understand the theoretical complexities of media production and circulation.

THE IDENTIFICATION OF A SUITABLE PEDAGOGY

If media education seriously intends to foster a critical awareness which enables children to filter meanings for themselves then it is more than the manifest curriculum which is at stake. Marshall McLuhan's now somewhat hackneyed phrase 'the medium is the message'[30] is as pertinent when applied to classroom pedagogy as it is to mass communication media. For, although the transmission of curriculum content may be the conscious intention of the teacher, the medium through which this is conveyed carries equal if not more powerful messages and in doing so becomes part of the content. Pedagogy wraps itself in a cocoon of subject matter and classroom routines until it becomes invisible and passively accepted by pupils and teachers alike, and in this unconscious form it is able to transmit educational and social ideology both effectively and silently. Because media education cannot afford the burden of a counter-productive hidden curriculum it is vital that the learning and evaluation procedures and classroom power relations are exposed, scrutinised and modified where necessary so that teaching methods work in harmony with the subject matter.

Media teachers need to accept from the beginning that their role is not that of dispensers or definers of knowledge; rather they should seek out what the children already understand and then organise the learning activities so as to extend and deepen this understanding. Once this has been accepted and the curriculum content negotiated, it is still necessary to examine the actual pedagogy because even within the accepted guidelines of good primary practice it is still possible for the teacher to retain control, not merely over the direction of the subject matter, but also over the classroom procedures which position the pupils as powerless and the teacher as controller and evaluator of the knowledge which the children need to 'discover' for themselves. Constantly the teacher needs to ask 'What do these children need in order to develop into self-motivated critical consumers of media products and fully literate citizens of the twenty-first century' and 'Does the pedagogy complement or conflict with this goal and is it conducive to fostering the growth of an on-going learning process which is both liberating and dynamic enough to endure rapid technological progress and survive "future shock"[31]?'.

The organisation of activity groups

An important element of media education is that it should actively position the learners on the inside of the processes of mediation so that reflection on these processes can form the basis for dialogue. Therefore the subject involves a great deal of practical and group work. Wherever possible the social construction of the groups should be such that all children are able to share their opinions and value those of others.

Simulation exercises

As a method of teaching, simulation exercises are of major importance in media education. By creating realistic activities which cast the pupils as media professionals it is possible to question the processes with first-hand experience. The intention is to make the scenario as life-like as possible and pupils must make decisions independently of the teacher, who organises the exercise but often takes no part in the action, although she may play a facilitating role. For instance, the pupils do not take on the role of journalists or advertisers; they *become* journalists or advertisers and, even though their achievements may be amateurish, the decision-making processes involved are precisely those of the professional.[32]

The first time a teacher organises a simulation she may experience an uncomfortable lack of control over what is happening in the classroom as she is temporarily redundant and the pupils often ignore her presence. Power relations have shifted. Using this teaching strategy it is possible to create, for quite young children, highly specific and relevant approaches to complex fundamental issues without claiming that they are definitive and closed learning exercises.

Reflective dialogue

Practical work is valuable only if it contributes to the child's ability to read media texts more critically. For instance, often vital connections between a news simulation exercise and an actual television broadcast are not so obvious to primary school children as might at first appear. Therefore, to prevent such activities degenerating into fragmented 'busy work', usually it is advisable to spend time helping the children to reflect on their experiences and make connections by means of group dialogue. It is important that the pupils are informed why they are learning about the media and how the understandings they gain can help them take control of their own lives, how they may gain access to the media and how their pleasures can be enhanced. A central goal of media education is to promote independence from the teacher so that critical autonomy is developed; consequently the sooner the children can take responsibility for their own learning the better it will be. Therefore it is useless for teachers to dominate discussions. Rather they need to encourage the children to express their own ideas and listen with courtesy to the opinions of their peers.

Cooperation versus competition

Central to the philosophy of media education is the need to value and draw upon the opinions and experiences of pupils. It follows then that group members must respect and cooperate with each other and this is not feasible if a competitive environment is fostered by the pedagogical stance of the teacher. It should be stressed to the children that an activity will not necessarily yield a finished and polished product, but rather it is an experiential, on-going process. For example, if the children have been working in groups, simulating a radio news broadcast and taping it, it should be made clear that there is something to be learned from all the tapes; there is no perfect tape, just different tapes. By minimising the need to compete, either individually or in groups, we can diminish the children's fear of failure and can prevent them from focusing on how their work may be assessed by the teacher or how it may be compared with the work of others.

CODA

The main aim of this book is to provide suggestions for primary school practice. Consequently the overview of the theoretical and historical basis of media studies has been, necessarily, brief. I hope, however, that this introduction will signpost and clarify some of the approaches which the practical chapters provide and so make it easier to explain our teaching to interested colleagues and parents.

Chapter 2

Teaching visual literacy

Humankind lingers unregenerately in Plato's cave, still reveling, its age old habit, in mere images of the truth. But being educated by photographs is not like being educated by older, more artisanal images. For one thing, there are a great many more images around, claiming our attention.[1]

THE NATURE OF VISUAL LITERACY: A DEFINITION OF THE QUEST

All images have the ability to transmit powerful and often unconscious messages through a culturally complicated system of signs and symbols, but their interpretation 'is not a question of mechanically reacting to stimuli'[2]; rather the receiver must learn to read the signs. A child's perception of these signs and symbols is socially determined and by the time she has entered the primary school her image vocabulary is extensive. For example, most primary school children recognise that the genre of cartoon signifies that any violence which is portrayed is unreal, and that the images immediately communicate to re-assure.[3] As Hodge and Tripp point out, the very large gap between the fantastic nature of cartoons and reality prevents any confusion.

If such learning is not to be a passive experience, then wher-ever possible the cognitive process should be raised to con-sciousness. Young children's interpretations have been shown to be highly complex but different from those of adults,[4] and Hodge and Tripp produced evidence which suggested that, although up to the age of 12 the development of children's cognitive and semiotic systems causes this difference in re-sponse, 'by the age of nine they are capable of their own kind of understanding of most mainstream television'.[5] It is not my intention to imply that children's responses to, and making sense of, television and other mass media are somehow inferior to those of adults. On the contrary I would suggest that every-one needs to learn how to read images critically. At this juncture I am reminded of the seminal article by Mezirow, *Perspective Transformations*, which proposes that adults returning to edu-cation must learn how they 'are caught in their own history and are reliving it'.[6] We all need to claim a fresh perspective on our social roles so that we can fulfil our potential. Consequently, I would wish to argue that it is important for children to be taught, early on in their school lives, how to analyse and con-front their own existing image vocabulary, for 'if we do not attempt to engage in an active reading of the images around us, we will tend to be seduced by a definition of the real world over which we have no control' and 'so we may become the way we see'.[7]

Many contemporary scholars have contributed to the debate which suggests that the criteria for literacy should be redefined so that they include the visual media,[8] and the arguments are often cogent if somewhat esoteric. However, for the purposes of this book the term 'visual literacy' simply indicates the skill which enables a reader to understand how meanings are written into an image and then how to question the interpretations which are evoked. An important step towards promoting visual literacy is for teachers to make seeing problematic for their pupils and then to devise approaches which equip children with the ability to review their own perceptions and break through the images to reveal deeper cultural, sociological and ideological messages.

PRACTICAL APPROACHES

Perception exercises

A simple way of problematising images is to present the children with a selection of ambiguous and puzzling pictures and optical illusions. Good sources for these are *The Anatomy of Judgement* by M.L.J. Abercrombie,[9] R.L. Gregory's *Eye and Brain*[10] and the illustrations of M.C. Escher, many of which are discussed in the intriguing book *Adventures with Impossible Figures* by Bruno Ernst.[11]

The organised structure of the children's past experiences – which Piaget called their 'schemata' – predisposes them to perceive the images in ways which make sense. The individual child's schemata represents her whole world of information and determines how she will be able to respond to, and interpret, visual information. A class exercise to demonstrate this process would be to show half of the class a card carrying the letters R S T U and the other half a card showing the numerals I II III IV and then to ask the whole class to interpret the same sign V.

Working in groups or pairs, to consider the meanings of the images, the children soon realise that not everyone can agree on what they mean but, by discussing the problems amongst themselves and with the help of the teacher, they can begin to understand how their preconceptions determine what they see. The intention is to teach the children to start questioning their own abilities to perceive 'correctly' and to accommodate this questioning stance into their existing schemata. Bruner said that

> once society has patterned man's interest and trained him what is likely in that society, it has gained a great measure of control not only on his thought processes but also on the very material on which thought works – the experienced data of perception.[12]

Very quickly the children recognise that images can often be ambiguous and exert influence, especially when they realise that sensory input sometimes cannot be decoded by the brain,

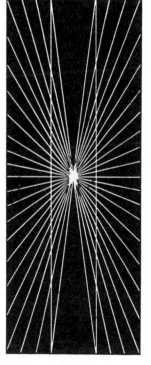

Block out A and C – the central figure is read as 13. Block out 12 and 14 – it is now read as B.

(Herring, 1861)

Old woman or young girl?

(Zollner, 1860)

Figure or background?

The Müller-Lyer illusion

Lift the page up and down and
moving radii will be seen
(S. P. Thompson, 1876)

for instance the visual dilemmas which pose as 3D constructions but which are feasible only in 2D.

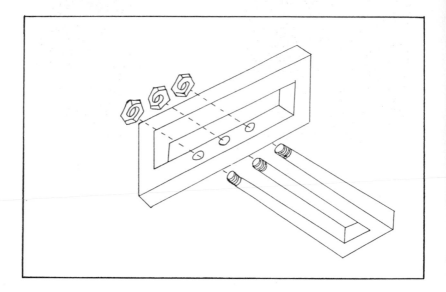

To illustrate the highly selective nature of everyday perception, have the children describe, without looking at an actual coin, both sides of a 10 pence piece, or if it is possible ask them to identify the correct drawing from a number of images of which only one is accurate.

Reviewing the familiar

During an art lesson ask the children to draw a familiar object – first from a conventional viewpoint and then from one which is selected to mislead the viewer. A light bulb drawn from a foreshortened perspective or a side view of a framed photo-graph makes it difficult to recognise these everyday articles. Another effective and enjoyable activity is to have the pupils work in pairs or groups to create a visual quiz using a camera to photograph, from unusual angles, items from in and around the classroom. The children will need to frame their subject care-fully in the viewfinder. By doing this they will be learning to select and manipulate the images to their own use – that is to say, to confound the viewer. When the photographs have been printed it is possible to make the puzzles harder by cropping them (cutting them down) to make the image selection more precise, or by mounting the pictures on their sides or inverted.

Naturally the pupils will want to experiment with their puzzles and the following suggestions may prove useful. The children can present their pictures to others in the school after predicting which age groups they think will find it easiest to recognise the objects. A scientifically fair test can be devised which will result in objective data. These data can be collected and converted into histograms, pie-charts, stick graphs and so on. All of this involves a considerable amount of cooperation and discussion of such variables as: how long should each child be allowed to view the photograph; is it fair to allow infants longer than third-year juniors; can the viewers hold the pictures themselves; should the tester put the children at their ease whilst they look, and so on? In addition to achieving the major objective of promoting visual literacy, this activity creates opportunities for social, aesthetic, mathematical, linguistic and scientific learning.

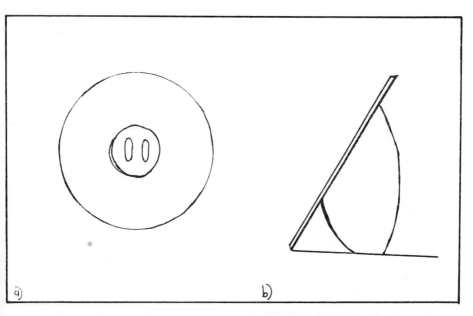

(a) Light bulb and (b) framed picture by Lee Wheatcroft, age 10

Throughout these initial explorations of images it is important to bear in mind that the learning is related to understanding how media products communicate. It is useful to make reference to how both still and moving pictures are decoded on the basis of the viewer's previous knowledge and to point out that visual communication is not simple and unlearnt but rather that it is our familiarity with visual conventions which shapes our interpretations. This familiarity can be explained by comparing it to the manner in which we make sense of the artistic technique of perspective. Railway lines appear to converge in the distance, mighty trees are drawn smaller than delicate flowers in order to signify that they are further away, and so on. Today we all accept this, but other cultures in earlier times have managed perspective very differently from ourselves. For example, the pictures created by the ancient Egyptians required that everything included in the picture should be seen from its most characteristic viewpoint.[13]

Completing the picture

The tendency of the brain to complete images in order to make sense of them can be exploited in a way which reinforces the learning that interpretations are rarely or never uniform. Copies of the cartoon opposite of a cleaning lady with her bucket can be given to the children for them to discuss, complete and colour. The finished pictures are usually widely different.

Progressing from this activity the teacher can prepare some cards similar to those on p. 32. Here the ambiguity lies in the lack of detail.[14]

Such partial images can be used as starting points with a whole class in order to compare the common visual stimulus with the multitude of possible closures which the children can suggest. Alternatively, working independently, each child in the class is given the same picture or pictures to complete and the work can be displayed as a frieze and used as a basis for reflective dialogue.

After taking part in this activity the children can begin to understand that, although we may be sure of the actual stimulus, the organisational patterns and filters of the mind are unique, so no one can be certain how another human being is reading an image. Already children will have developed atti-

tudes, values and interests which coax them into perceiving what they are looking for and rejecting what is not expected or hoped for in an image. How many goal posts were seen in image Number 1 on p. 32?

Eye witness

Using a drama/role play lesson, have the children work in pairs or small groups to create a scene from everyday school life which is able to be photographed from two viewpoints each of which tells a different story. For example, the girl and boy in the pictures on p. 33 were 'playing' a game but the girl's expression of intense concentration, if seen without her opponent and the chessboard, could be decoded as anger.

When a collection of these pairs of viewpoint photographs has been produced it is fun for the children to show them to other classes to supply short interpretative commentaries for each photograph. If the pairs of photographs are displayed, together with their commentaries, it makes an enjoyable centre of interest which motivates critical awareness.

A slight variation on this activity is to ask the children to

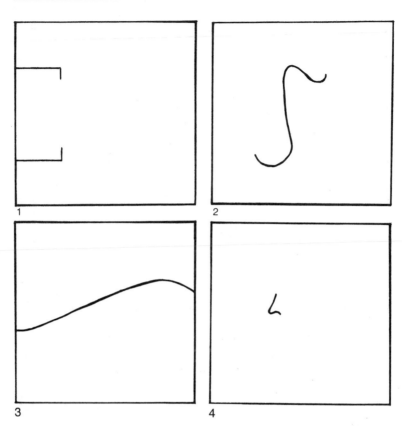

photograph a familiar scene using different camera angles. For instance, take a picture of the head teacher's desk first from a kneeling position and then from a high angle (have the child stand on a chair). Such photographs can be used to stimulate discussion about how the impressions which are evoked by a scene can be altered by changing the position of the camera.

Framed

The following activity is valuable in any situation where we want the children to experiment with techniques of visual editing. First choose some pictures – they can be amateur photographs, newspaper pictures, advertisements, posters or anything. When the size of the picture is known, make a series of three or more frames each increasingly smaller than the

original picture. The idea is to place the least revealing frame over the picture and ask the children what they can say about the meaning of the image. Frame 1 is replaced by frame 2 and the children once again are asked to interpret what is now visible. The process is repeated with frame 3 and finally with no frame at all. Naturally as the children see more, their perceptions of the situation increase. The final question is – what has been excluded from the photograph which could have made the viewer's understanding more complete?[15]

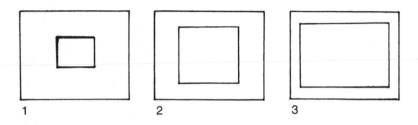

1   2   3

Every picture tells a story

To answer this question have each girl and boy in the class bring a photograph to school. Preferably the picture should be one which features the child on holiday or in a familial situation. Blu-tack this photograph to a piece of A3 paper and ask the owner to extend the image. The individual knowledge which each child possesses about the scene enables him or her to draw in other characters and background details which allow the viewers to make greater sense of the picture. When this art activity is completed have the pupil write an account of what the photograph means and this can be displayed alongside the extended picture when the next part of the activity has been accomplished. This involves removing each photograph from the centre of the drawing, photocopying it and replacing each picture with its copy. The original photograph can now be fixed into the centre of a fresh sheet of A3 paper and the exercise repeated, but this time by a different child, preferably one who has not seen the drawing by the photograph's owner. It emerges that each picture tells a story but it is not the same story to all viewers.

Posed and candid pictures

A photograph's intrinsic potential for transmitting meanings is shared between the subject and the photographer but the control is rarely divided equally. An activity which helps children to recognise how this power is allotted is to explore the differences between posed and unposed pictures. Make a collection of photographs which depict people. Once again the pictures should be from a variety of sources. After they have divided them into two sets – posed and unposed – the children should be asked to describe the ways in which the two sets are distinguished. To facilitate their thinking the suggestions in Worksheet 1 may help. A large sheet of paper may be divided into two and the children can create a collage, with one half of the paper containing posed pictures and the other half displaying unposed.

Worksheet 1

1 Which set of pictures has the most close-ups/smiling faces?
2 Draw some speech bubbles and write in what the people are saying/thinking.
3 Which kinds of photographs are nearly always posed/unposed?
4 Take a camera onto the playground at break-time and take some pairs of pictures. The first of each pair should be a quick snapshot of a group of children playing. Ask the same group of children to pose whilst a second, 'action' photograph is taken of their game.

Family photographs: snap happy

In order to examine some of the common visual codes of the photographic image, have the children bring to school as many photographs of themselves and their families as they can find. There is usually no shortage, especially if it is stressed that 'failure photographs' are welcome. Sometimes the children bring the pictures in the envelopes in which they were originally collected from the shop. The commercially produced 'snapshots' that feature on these envelopes are worth comparing with the photographs which we, as amateurs, produce. After making a collection of the photographs, divide the class into groups.

Give each group a random selection of photographs and ask for these to be put into sets. Usually the groups find that the pictures fall into readily recognisable categories: holiday time, Christmas, birthdays, and so on. Pets, children and grandparents are the favourite subjects and it is rare to find a photograph without a human or an animal posing for the camera. Both the occasions and the subjects are carefully selected and because we require happy memories which meet our emotional needs, people are invariably pictured smiling and with their arms around each other. We have lots of new baby pictures in the family album but a funeral is never featured, yet it records our family history just as significantly. However, the universally recorded smile is frequently far from a reflection of reality and it is interesting to have the children describe what happened both prior to the picture's being taken and afterwards. Often it is useful to ask who the photographer was, as this can influence the choice of subject. Mostly the images are selected to signify happiness, family well-being, friendship, and the unseen photographers have been engaged in building codes which they know will shape the viewer's impressions.

Reading images of family history

Many of the children have access to family photographs which were taken earlier this century and if these are borrowed and displayed it is possible to contrast them with photographs taken today. The children's analyses of the pictures can be guided by a series of structured questions similar to those in Worksheets 2 and 3 which relate to the pictures on pp. 38 and 39 respectively.

In her Channel 4 publication *The Family Album*, Sue Isherwood suggests that, by talking to the various people who remember the photograph's being taken or, failing this, to those who might know something of the biography of the people depicted, it is possible to show how

> a single image can be a focal point of a cluster of conflicting memories and knowledge but [that] these different readings do not necessarily cancel one another out, rather they reveal the complexity of what an image can tell us – and what it can't.[16]

Once the initial analyses of the pictures are completed, the children can be encouraged to discuss the photographs with

Worksheet 2 (see picture A overleaf)

1 *How old is this picture? Give three reasons for your guess.*
2 *What relation to the bride is the little girl who is sitting nearest to her and why is there a circle round the child's head?*
3 *Who are the other childen?*
4 *Why is the picture taken at the back of a house rather than at a church or registry office?*
5 *Is it summer or winter?*
6 *Are the people rich or poor? How can you tell?*
7 *Which flowers are used to make the bride's bouquet?*
8 *What are the chains which are hanging across the men's waistcoats?*
9 *What do you think is in the boxes which are being carried by the bridesmaids?*
10 *What kinds of jobs do you think that the grown-ups do?*
11 *Why are the people in this group looking so serious?*
12 *Make up a story telling what has happened to one of these children on this day.*

Worksheet 3 (see picture B overleaf)

1 *Where was this little boy when this picture was taken?*
2 *What is the mark underneath the photograph? [N.B. Van Ralty Ltd was a well-known and fashionable photographic studio]*
3 *Describe the child's clothes.*
4 *How does this picture differ from a modern photograph?*
5 *Where would a picture like this be placed?*

their families (bearing in mind that we may need to exercise tact). In addition to being an excellent use of the skill of listening and speaking, it should help establish that it is legitimate for an image to have multiple interpretations.

Stories in pictures

Examining a single still image can be challenging, but if a second picture is placed before or after it then the reading of the image becomes a far more complex process. A picture of a busker

A

B

entertaining a theatre queue followed by a photograph of a police constable may signify that the busker is to be moved on. If this second picture were to be replaced by one showing the same busker on a popular television show, the meaning would be entirely different. Film and television constantly demand that we make sense of the juxtapositioning of images and it is important that we put children on the inside of such editing procedures.

One way to approach this learning is to suggest that the children work in groups to create a simple story which can be told in photographs. Each group should collaborate to produce a simple storyboard. A storyboard is a series of pictures and instructions which show how a narrative, usually in the medium of film, is to be portrayed. Each frame of the storyboard illustrates a key moment in the drama and allows space to include a description of the action and the dialogue. Sometimes it is relevant to include sound effects, music, camera angles and other details. To save effort it is a good idea to give younger children prepared blank storyboards (see p. 41).

When these are completed the story can be photographed. Every frame will require the pupils to select visual codes and camera angles, to decide what needs to be included or excluded to make the meaning clear and also to consider how the image will be read by the audience. Although the narratives must be simple they will all still need an establishing shot to lead the reader into the story, a disruption of harmony, a closing device and so on. By photographing their own stories the children become unavoidably implicated in the process of constructing images which rely on body language, facial expression and other visual conventions. They also develop an awareness that it is possible to make the camera lie by employing techniques such as montage. For example, when a group of 9 year olds, who were in my class, were photographing their story, which was about a boy who kicked a ball onto our school roof (not an acceptable activity), they created a montage sequence of three pictures which they hoped produced a convincing visual deceit:

1. a medium-shot depicting a group of children playing with a football in the playground;
2. a close-up image of a boy's foot kicking a ball;
3. a long-shot showing the children pointing angrily at the school roof.

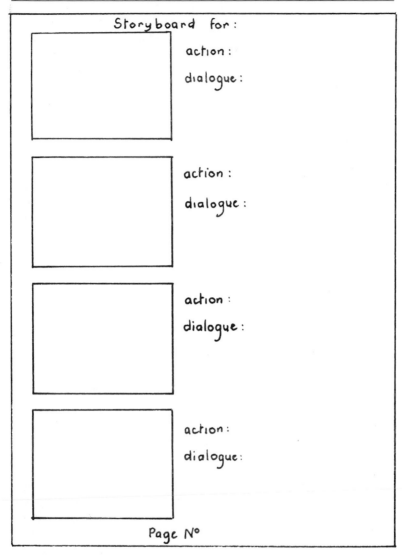

The children had recognised that a close-up shot's 'meaning is largely parasitic upon those images which surround it'.[17]

Another group of 8 year olds created a story about a sapling developing into a fully grown tree. First they photographed the tiny plant; their second picture showed a calendar; image number three was of a young tree; the fourth picture depicted the calendar two years later; and so on. Time had passed. By

talking about these conventions of visual editing which they had already absorbed from their own experiences of media consumption, the children were able to understand more of the ways in which meaning is written into moving images and how audience reactions can be influenced. Gradually, that which is often invisible becomes visible and in clearer focus and, as it does so, it brings to birth a new generation of questions.

When the picture stories are developed and printed there are many valuable learning activities which can be explored. Each group of children can swap sets of pictures to see if the stories are always decoded in the same ways that they were encoded. The pupils can resequence their own photographs to create a different narrative. Sets of pictures can be combined and new stories created. All of the photographs may be placed face downwards on a table and shuffled; random pairs can then be turned over and made sense of together so that the children can discuss how different readings may emerge from the same images and how this depends on the context as well as the content.

Comics, clues and codes

Even in the era of soap operas, satellite TV, pop videos and interactive computer games, comics are still part of young people's popular culture and may provide a valuable, non-threatening introduction to many of the key issues in visual literacy. Without realising it, the children have learnt to understand quite a complex and specific system of non-verbal communication through their reading of comic strips. The vast majority of 7 year olds have no difficulty in identifying the meaning of signs such as these when they are read in the context of a comic:

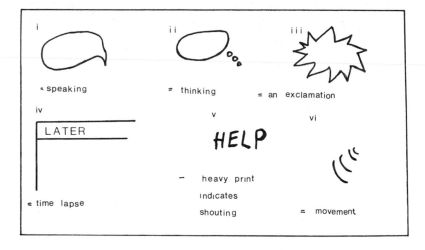

Once the codes have been learnt they become an accepted part of the narrative structure of the comic and it is this structure which, to a large extent, prompts the children's expectations.

After discussing with the class how a few of these signs operate in the comic strip, ask the pupils to work in pairs or small groups to see how many others they can find in their favourite comics. The children will frequently discover more than we expect and this search often leads them to examine how onomatopoeic words are employed, usually to great effect, in the medium.

As each sign within an image depends for its meaning on its relationship with other signs the children need to be encouraged to look at the pictures in great detail, discuss with their group how the codes operate and perhaps experiment by changing parts of the drawing to see if this changes the overall meaning. How the signs work within the whole narrative can be demonstrated by a range of resequencing games, cloze procedures and prediction exercises.[18]

A particularly effective activity can be created by cutting some comic stories into individual frames, shuffling these and asking the children to work in groups to resequence them. (Although initially time consuming, I found that it was ultimately worthwhile mounting all of the exercises described here onto card, covering them with sticky-backed plastic, numbering them to avoid mixing them up and then storing them in labelled envelopes.) To enable the children to articulate and become conscious of their learning Worksheet 4 may help.

Worksheet 4

1 *Put this comic strip back into the original order.*
2 *When you have completed the task, write down a list of clues which helped you.*
3 *Now try to make another story with these same pictures. Try to create a different ending. (You need not use all of the frames this time.)*

For the prediction exercise, the final frame is removed from the page and the children are asked to work in groups to guess how the story ends and draw their own last picture. For the cloze procedure, a frame is removed from anywhere within the storyline and the pupils have to imagine what it consisted of. Once this exercise has been accomplished, the groups can be required to produce several alternative completing frames and say why some of these are likely or unlikely solutions.

A different kind of prediction exercise may be produced by blocking out the comic strip speech bubbles (or some of them) and making enough copies for a whole class so that they can work in pairs or small groups to fill in the dialogue. (I have found that it helps greatly if the size of the page is enlarged when it is reproduced, as very young children find it difficult to make their writing small enough to fit into the bubbles.) For this task the students must make sense of the images, discuss how characters are expected to behave, and work logically from

frame to frame modifying their predictions in the light of possibly conflicting evidence. When all of the children have finished
the activity it is essential that each group shares its results with
others in the class for, although the stories are usually very
predictable, there are often many intriguing variations. A display panel of the completed stories acts like a magnet even for
pupils who have reading difficulties. By experiencing this
activity, once again the children realise that a story can be
decoded very differently depending on the viewpoint of the
reader.

Semiology and image

Once we have begun labouring at extracting the meaning from
an image it becomes apparent that this is a complex process
which obliges us to consider how clothes, body language, cultural artefacts and so on are able to signify a wealth of important
information. An effective introduction to semiology (the science
of signs and how and why meanings are attached to things) is to
provide the children with newspapers and magazines from
which they can clip pictures of a wide variety of people which
can be categorised and made into collages. The categories could
include: female/male pop stars, mothers, politicians, soldiers,
football supporters, young children. In this way clusters of signs
which help us to identify the categories become more visible.
There is no natural relationship between footwear, make-up,
jewellery, clothes, cars or even words and what they mean, but
they are all communications that are generally accepted and that
signify meaning in culturally powerful ways. Hairstyles,
fashions and cult possessions such as skateboards and moun-
tain bikes become increasingly important to both boys and girls
as they pass through their junior school years, and a class
discussion can reveal just what the current styles signify.

   Another activity which illustrates how symbols (those signs
which are considered to be especially rich in meaning) can be
effective as communication tools is to ask the children to draw
and then deconstruct some of their club emblems. A rugby club
which a boy in my class attended sported a black and yellow
striped badge which featured a tiger. He told me that this
signified the ferocity with which the team played. Once the
pupils understand how symbolism operates they can create

shields which are symbolic of their families; they may wish to incorporate their names, the number of people in the household, the colours of their car and house, and so on. In this simple way the children gain an insight into how visual communications are culturally connected with all aspects of meaning. Two booklets by Andrew Bethell[19] provide teachers with many similar activities which can be adapted for use in the primary classroom.

Cultural artefacts

The messages of visual codes have many levels of meaning but unpeeling these with young children is not as difficult as might be supposed. Masterman[20] demonstrates how secondary pupils can be asked to describe an artefact at a denotative level, then tease out the connotations from this description and finally identify the network of signs which show how the object is the result of historical and culturally based human choices which represent social values. The activity can quite easily be attempted by primary children and preparatory class discussions usually reveal just how perceptive these children can be.

Daniel (age 10), when describing his key-ring, suggested that the object would be redundant in a society that was neither possessive nor dishonest. A sports trophy yielded other cultural revelations to this same class: it signified that competition is generally a socially acceptable norm, that success leads to tangible, extrinsic rewards and that sporting achievements are the subject of public pride.

Recently I tried this activity with a class of vertically grouped first- and second-year juniors. In dialogue, it was possible for the children to understand the terms 'culture' and 'cultural'; as one girl put it, 'culture is what humans create – it's the opposite of natural'. After the whole class had contributed to the scrutiny of a pound coin, each child chose an object to describe. This is what Stephen wrote about his digital watch.

It is black, in the middle the [sic] is a hexagon, with a grey bit in the middle. In the grey bit some sticks dance about. There are some shapes dotted around the grey bit, with blue lines around it. There are three silver prongs sticking out from the sides, two on the left hand side, one on the right. At the top and bottom there are black strips going down. They are wide at the roots and thin at the end. One strip has holes in it, the other has a sliding bit on it. The hexagon is 3 cm wide and its overall lenght [sic] is 23 cm. A watch in our society means we like to know the time, and other things like when it is time to do something, or have lunch. This signifies we like to be aware of things so that we can make the most of our time.

(Stephen Boothroyd, age 8)

At this very simple level children can begin to demythologise cultural objects to reveal ideological messages which have been cloaked in what Barthes referred to as 'naturalness';[21] a naturalness that suppresses politics and history, both of which need to be reasserted. For Barthes the pseudo-openness of the language of myth blinds us to its ideological potential and it operates in a parasitic way to distort and obliterate the truth only to redefine it in its own terms. Because myth and the media are both transmitters of culture and because 'technology itself is also part of the taken for granted world',[22] it is important that children appreciate how they can apply this demythologising technique to media products – not simply to demystify them but to enrich the understanding and enjoyment they derive from them.

It is a relatively easy step to link the learning of how cultural objects signify meaning to how media environments, for instance, can guide responses. Try looking at a variety of television programmes and considering what the background and general setting are leading us to expect. The formally dressed, carefully spoken newsreader seated behind a desk is suggestive of a serious, truthful, informative broadcast, whereas a character in a pink suit carrying a ridiculous puppet informs us that the subject matter of the programme is to be amusing and trivial. Even more significant is the fact that the actual medium of television demands that we learn to unravel particular technological codes. Justin Lewis discusses this need when he describes a televised cricket match.

> The mysterious voice from somewhere out of the picture we are able, as well trained TV watchers, to understand as the voice of a 'commentator'. The fact that the men in white appear and disappear quite suddenly, simultaneously growing or shrinking, does not contravene the laws of science. To

the trained viewer, such abnormalities appear quite natural –
we *know* that TV broadcasts can switch from one camera to
another and we are *used* to seeing it that way[23].

Animation

Making the transition from exploring still pictures to television's
continuous stream of images is a very necessary step in the
development of visual literacy. With primary children a pleasur-
ably simple introduction to this is to create flip books and to
enjoy making some optical toys such as zoetropes, phenakisto-
scopes and thaumatropes which were popular in the nineteenth
century. (Instructions for making these, together with examples
and simple histories, can be purchased very cheaply.[24])

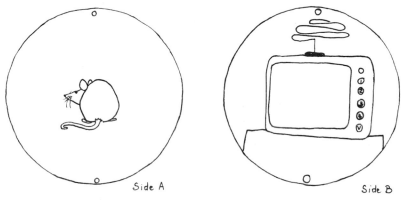

Side A   Side B

The intention is to show how the eye takes a mere fraction of a
second to register an image with the brain and that, if slightly
different still images are seen in rapid succession, they appear as
if they were moving. This scientific fact can be demonstrated
easily by making a thaumatrope. To do this cut a circle out of
thin card and draw an image on side A; on side B draw a
complementary image. Cut a small hole at the top and the
bottom of the circle and to each of these attach a piece of string.
Have a child hold each end of the string and ask one of them to
twist the thread. When this is released the thaumatrope spins
and the two images appear as one.

In the early part of this century thaumatropes were sometimes
made out of gold and worn as ornaments on the watch chains.

My grandfather (featured in the wedding photograph in this chapter) wore such a thaumatrope. This had the top half of the letters of the word 'love' inscribed on one side and on the reverse side it had the bottom part of the letters. Children can try writing their names in this way.

An alternative and very simple activity is to make a roller picture. On two identical pieces of paper draw the same image but have these differing slightly. Superimpose the papers and hinge them together at one end. Curl the top sheet round a pencil and then move the pencil backwards and forwards so that the image is seen to move.

For those teachers wishing to develop the theme of animation further, two teaching packs, together with a video, have been produced by the Arts Council for use in the primary classroom.[25]

Writing with light

Before concluding this chapter on visual literacy it is worth saying a little about the valuable contribution that working with light-sensitive paper can bring. Quite understandably many teachers voice the concerns that the chemicals are dangerous, that the equipment is expensive and that the skills are too complicated for very young children. These statements are not necessarily true and the excitement and valuable cross-curricular learning which are generated by the activities more than compensate for any difficulties. Moreover, if we wish to enable children to look critically at photographic images, surely we should be teaching them how they are created. There are many excellent books which explain the techniques, – perhaps the most accessible of which is the *Ilford Manual of Classroom Photography*.[26] However, for those wishing to experiment let me explain one of the activities – the making of photograms – which has captivated the interest of all the 7–10 year olds with whom I have tried it.

The basic requirements for creating photograms are: four shallow dishes (old trays from children's tables are ideal so long as they are water tight), a red safety light (this can be a torch with the reflector removed and the glass covered with a piece of red gel), a light source (a torch or Anglepoise lamp would be fine), rubber gloves and/or tongs, photographic paper, developer and fixer, a piece of string and some laundry pegs, and a room from which the light has been excluded – we used an old changing room. The four trays should be clearly labelled developer (alkaline), stop-bath (mild acid), fixer (acid) and water, respectively, and placed in this order on a table. The developer and fixer should be mixed as indicated on the containers and the children should be warned that these are dangerous. To protect their clothing from spillages it is wise for them to wear art overalls. There is no need to buy a stop-bath chemical as it can be created by adding a few drops of vinegar to a tray of water. The light source and the closed box of photographic paper should be placed on a different table. The children then need to make collections of suitable objects – ideally there should be a mixture of opaque, transparent and translucent things. Leaves, key-rings, paper clips, rulers, paper doillies, shells, combs, jewellery, light bulbs, flowers are all perfect candidates.

With white light excluded from the room and the red safety light switched on, one sheet of paper can now be removed from the box. Make sure that the children know that they must put the paper away and close the box securely before the white light is put on or all of the paper will be ruined. The chosen object or objects are placed on the light-sensitive side of the paper and exposed to light for a few seconds. (Later on it is possible to experiment by shining the light onto the paper from different angles to produce different effects.) The paper is then placed in the developer and agitated for about 1½ minutes. The children must use rubber gloves and it is recommended that they also use tongs to pick the paper out of the chemicals. Once the image has emerged satisfactorily, the paper should be removed from the developer, placed into the stop-bath for 1 minute and then placed in the fixer for a further minute. Lastly put it into the fourth dish of clean water. When all of the children's prints have been made they should be washed for 2 minutes in running water and hung to dry on a washing line.

I have found it profitable to introduce the class to the whole process in the form of a dry run, and then have the pupils work in the dark room in small groups with a responsible parent helper. Obviously this is just one activity using light-sensitive paper and it may be extended in many ways.

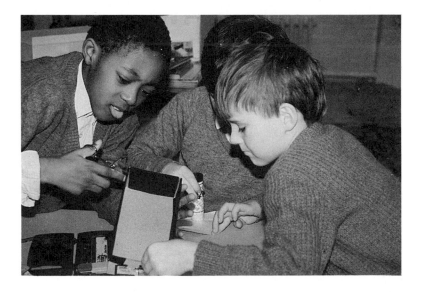

For instance, the children can make pin-hole cameras with which they can take photographs. To do this, in addition to the materials needed for the production of photograms, you will need: a container with a tightly fitting lid (a shoe box may be suitable), some non-reflective black paper or paint, a piece of kitchen foil, a sheet of glass, a piece of card and some adhesive tape. Completely cover the inside of the container with black paper or paint and cut a hole about 1 cm square in the centre of one side. Cover this with kitchen foil and make a hole in it with a pin. Next make a flap of card which will cover the hole and fix it in position with a hinge of adhesive tape. Also put a piece of tape to hold the bottom of it temporarily in position. In a dark room, with the red light on, remove the lid and, with the emulsion side facing, place a piece of photographic paper on the side of the box facing the hole and secure the lid with tape. The camera is now ready to take the picture.

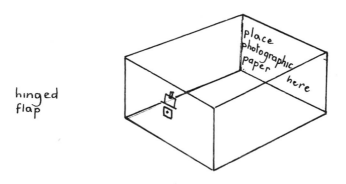

It is wise to choose an outside subject which is unlikely to move; a tree, a building or a group of stationary children are suitable. Steady the camera on a wall or table about 5–10 metres away, lift the cardboard hinge to reveal the pinhole for about 2 minutes, then tape the hinge back in position. Obviously the exposure time will depend on the brightness of the day and how far the paper is away from the hole, so expect that it will take several attempts before the children get it correct.

In the dark room remove the paper and process it in the same way as for the photograms. If the paper has been exposed for too long it will go completely black when placed in the developer. After a successful image has been achieved the children will see that it is a negative. It is possible to produce a positive print. To do this take another piece of photographic paper and

put the negative face down onto it, place a piece of glass over both papers to keep them flat and then shine a light onto them. Now repeat the printing process.

CONCLUSION

'Seeing comes before words';[27] likewise it is being familiar with the processes involved in visual communication which is important. Primary children should not necessarily be expected to articulate, in general terms, the new awarenesses which will have been raised by their explorations in visual literacy. It is the ability to connect them with specific media texts which is essential. Therefore it matters that the activities suggested in this chapter are related to the children's own experiences and, where it is appropriate, to their current media interests. No book or pack of teaching resources can do this because only the teacher knows the unique needs and interests of her class.

Teaching visual literacy is not an easy task but, I believe, is one which is worthwhile in a world packed with images. It is logical to suppose that the child who, early on, is taught to read print effectively for meaning – searching for nuances and inferences and so on – will eventually become a better reader than she who is taught nothing but word recognition skills. A growth in the skill of visual literacy, like conventional literacy, should lead to an enhancement of the children's pleasure in reading the texts.

Chapter 3

Learning about news

News is the product of an organised process which entails a practical way of looking at events in order to tie them together, make simple and direct statements about their relationship, and to do this in an entertaining way.[1]

WHAT'S IN THE NEWS FOR US?

Because television, radio and newspapers inevitably need to select current affairs which they consider worthy of our attention and then construct stories in presentable ways, it is reasonable to infer that the media possess a measure of control over our knowledge and interpretation of national and international news events and issues. We accept that newspapers may be politically biased, but statistical evidence indicates that information which is received from television and radio news broadcasts is generally regarded as neutral or balanced.[2] It is expected that these programmes order and clarify events and issues. However, it is a media literacy skill to be aware of whose assumptions and values are maintaining the balance, clarifying the issues and structuring this order.

Although democratically valuable, to begin this learning in the primary school may seem ambitious. This is not necessarily so. Understanding how news is manufactured can be fostered at this level in ways which actively involve the children in the processes of mediation and, when pupils can relate to the subject matter, the work is popular. From the very start it must be stressed that this chapter is not about creating school newspapers (however worthwhile this may be in other contexts) or emulating other professional media; rather it is about children developing the skill of critical awareness, and this can mature only with practice. In my experience, primary students tend to complain that there is too much news on television and generally they find it hard to be interested in many of the complex political and social issues that underpin world events, which frequently occur in distant and, sometimes, unheard of locations. In addition we must bear in mind that research findings show that, as a matter of course, young children cease attending to news broadcasts as soon as the genre is recognised;[3] moreover, the newscaster's 'talking head' is another factor which causes pupils to remove their attention from the screen.[4] Therefore, although the precise learning outcomes cannot be predicted accurately, the approach must be carefully matched to the children's cognitive development so as to engage their interest and, what is more, the knowledge gained should be immediately useful and focus on their present consumption of news.

So, before starting classroom activities, it is a good plan to have the pupils watch some television news and then for the teacher to listen carefully to their reactions. Readers may be interested to compare what their children say with some of the responses my classes have made after watching a news broadcast.

Esther (11):	'. . . News is really for telling what's happening in life.'
Tony (11):	'They're telling people the facts.'
Brian (11):	'If it wasn't facts, why would they call it news?'
Esther:	'They showed you a clip . . . so you know it's the truth.'

Tony: 'It *was* news, it was for people to enjoy but it
               was telling you about about real things.'

               [Of BBC *Newsround*]
Brian: '*Newsround* is meant for kids.'
Laurence (11): 'There's not much violence.'
Tony: 'But it doesn't give you all the facts.'
Laurence: 'On *Newsround* they don't show you pictures of
               hurt people. On ITN they show you pictures of
               them all being killed and that.'

                              *   *   *

Arnold (9):   'If they didn't tell the truth everything would be
               wrong in the world, we wouldn't know any-
               thing. . . . We know it's true because you hear it
               on other programmes.'

                              *   *   *

Barry (7):   'It said *today* and they've got cameras . . . other
               programmes have *names* and are on once a week
               but *news* is on *everyday*, it's always on and it's on
               at certain times, but other programmes are on
               just one time.'

Although these children realised a news broadcast intended for
their age range would be expurgated, it was clear that they
recognised television news as a regular reliable service and one
which they believed merited very few questions. It simply
arrived in their homes like water, gas and electricity.[5]

PRACTICAL APPROACHES

Image and text

Once we begin to understand the children's attitudes towards
news, there are many simple introductory deconstructing activities from which to choose. Maybe one of the first tasks is to
separate text from pictures in order to comprehend how the
interpretation of an image is influenced by commentary.

Older juniors can be set the following task, which, like a
number of the other activities in this chapter, is derivative of

work which has been suggested for secondary school media studies courses.[6] At home or at school, using a variety of newspapers, each child selects and clips out a photograph, mounts it onto a piece of card and by the side of the picture writes the published caption. She now creates for herself a completely different but plausible caption, which is written on the other side of the photograph. I have found that if the children prepare the card at home their parents become involved and the adult contributions and the discussions which occur increase the value of the exercise. When all have prepared their cards these are displayed and the game is to guess which captions are the originals. Besides being fun, the children can appreciate how a text has the power to coax the reader into a 'preferred' interpretation of the image and that the photograph does not simply illustrate the words but rather that the words are often 'parasitic' upon it.[7]

An exercise which is effective with younger juniors is to present the pupils with a selection of newspaper photographs from which the accompanying text has been removed. The children can work individually or in pairs. Each child/pair takes a photograph and spends a pre-specified time (maybe 15 minutes) discussing the picture, deciding what it means, devising a catchy headline and then writing an interpretative account. After the allotted time they have to pass on their picture to another child/pair and the process is repeated. After they have all completed about four or five of these, mount the stories together with the matching picture. Usually the stories vary greatly. This activity aims to sow the seeds of doubt as to the certainty of interpreting images on the basis of text and to demonstrate that when commentary is stripped from the picture the interpretation ceases to be fixed.

Another approach to this concept is to ask the class to work in pairs or small groups and select some aspect of school life which, when photographed, would offer a favourable impression if seen in a local newspaper. The second part of this exercise is for each pair/group to repeat the task, but this time choosing a negative aspect. When the photographs are printed they should be mounted on card, numbered and passed around the class. Working in pairs the children write a negative and a positive headline to match each photograph, irrespective of the original intention of the photographer.

Stevenson School gets very untidy by the end of the week.

Stevenson School has lots of equipment and it is well used.

A news simulation

Having introduced the children to how text is able to attach particular significance to photographic images it is a good idea to devise an activity which relates to the more complex medium of television. The following news simulation may be adapted successfully for most primary pupils.

Take about twenty photographs around the school or maybe during a day trip. Perhaps these could illustrate a special event: a harvest festival, the carol service, sports day, the end of term, disruption from workmen mending the roof, are all suitable themes. Some commercially produced teaching packs include sets of pictures for such activities,[8] but, even though these are good, rarely are they as successful as the ones which you, the teacher, can make for your own class. It really is most important that young children are totally involved with the subject matter and this means that it must be recent and relevant to them and preferably in colour. Duplicate sets of the pictures need to be made but photocopies will suffice if this is too expensive. The children should work in mixed-ability groups of about five or six.

Worksheet 5

* You are a team of journalists wanting to make a short news item for tonight's local television news. It is about . . . [for example: the end of term at —— School]. You have just arrived back in the studio with the film (imagine that each photograph is a few seconds of film) you took on location at the school earlier today. Your job is to edit the film and write a script to go with it.
* You can choose about nine pictures (pieces of film) which tell the story well. Put these into a story order and Blu-tack them onto your card/ paper. Leave enough space under each picture so that you can write your commentary.
* Write the words you want to go with each picture.
* You have one hour to do all of this work and to practise saying it. Then you should be ready to go 'on air'.

Each group of children is given a complete set of pictures, some Blu-tack and a large sheet of card or paper and instructions similar to those in Worksheet 5. Obviously the task must be much simpler for the younger children; for instance, the commentary could be tape-recorded. With the older juniors the groups can be given different briefs which offer alternative slants to each story. This shows how the editor not only functions as a gatekeeper but also sets the agenda as to how the story should be interpreted. For example, with a class of children working on a news story about the end of term one group can be asked to say how it was chaotic, another group to show how unhappy everyone was to be leaving their old classes, a third may be briefed to say how delighted they all were to be having a long holiday. As a rule the children adhere to editorial wishes: like real journalists they need to please their superiors in order to have their stories printed/broadcast. No one writes what she knows will be rejected. Sometimes it is useful to allot tasks within the groups – scriptwriters, news reader, producer and so on. A further refinement to the simulation would be to exclude from the selection of photographs one image which depicts a centrally important feature of the event and see if the children feel that it is still worth mentioning when there is no picture to illustrate it. As with the ILEA teaching pack *Teachers' Protest*[9] (which is suitable only for older students), the simulation can be enhanced by obtaining slides of the images and projecting these onto a screen while the script is being read, rather than having the children hold up their completed work to show the rest of the class.

Once the simulation has started the children settle into their roles and the teacher is free to observe and act as adviser. The work is normally highly task orientated and as the deadline approaches it becomes feverish. When the stories are shown and the scripts read, it is usual for each group to discover that it has selected many of the same photographs as the other groups but that the commentaries anchor the meaning and persuade the viewer to interpret the images to signify different messages. The exercise goes some way to dispel the notion that a neutral position can ever be achieved and to impart the idea that the news is not the whole truth but a selection from the truth. The children will have experienced, from the very onset, how this selectivity is built into media representations and they will now begin to understand how it is that dominant social values and assumptions underlie this choice and how news offers us a particular set of guidelines for interpreting the world.

At some point it may be worth relating the widely known traditional Indian folk tale of the blind people who, after meeting and touching an elephant, were asked to describe it. To each person the elephant felt different: he who felt the tail said an elephant was like a piece of rope, the person handling the ear insisted that it was thin and flat, like a leaf, the one who felt the tusk assured the audience that an elephant was hard like a stone. They all 'saw' the elephant differently.

Simulation exercises usually engender cooperative group activity as there is little competition either within or between the groups. There are no right or wrong answers and the work is enjoyable. Nevertheless, we must not lose sight of the main purpose of the activity which is to create a basis for the promotion of critical thinking. From experience I have found that group reflection and dialogue after a simulation are vital in arousing and highlighting critical awareness. Usually the children have been able to garner enough knowledge to speak, or argue their cases, with authority and sometimes it is possible to raise issues which could not have been forecast accurately by the teacher. Once the simulation is completed it is necessary to

transform the children's experiences of the processes of mediation into a basis for generating media literacy skills. Sometimes
it is helpful to ask the pupils to write about their learning,
especially if the dialogue has facilitated the sharing of valuable
insights.

After such a dialogue this 10-year-old girl wrote:

> We found out how hard it is to select which bits of the film to
> use, which storys [sic] are the most important, that will
> entertain people so they don't switch off, which commentar-
> ies to write to go with the film. We also found how difficult it
> is to have to work to a deadline. It was hard to try to think
> about what was happening when the pictures were taken. It
> must be even harder for reporters to have to go perhaps to
> another country and report about something they don't even
> know. It was interesting to see how the pictures that we
> used, were used in a completely different way to mean some-
> thing very different. So we had written a biast [sic] story. It
> was a slightly different truth. Some people seemed to have
> their own opinions on the same subject. It was hard for me to
> write out all the writing with everybody fussing around me
> and arguing about which pictures to use. It really felt like we
> were in a newsroom. It felt like I was really a script writer
> working at Central. It was a very interesting experience. I
> think a producer's job would be one of the hardest.
>
> (Gemma Needham, age 10)

Reflective writing is often an aid to objectifying, clarifying and
heightening learning which has arisen from a practical
activity,[10] and in her writing Gemma was able to raise the level
of her own critical awareness and capture and articulate insights
which might otherwise have escaped and been forgotten.

That can't be me

Many of the children will have experienced their own exposure
to the media. Naturally they will have kept their cuttings, and if
they can be persuaded to bring these into school it provides an
opportunity to explore the accuracy of the articles. Recently
some of our pupils, who had contributed to a charitable event,
were featured in the local newspaper. In a hundred or so words
of copy the journalists had reported at least two incorrect facts

and spelt names wrongly. Furthermore, they had persuaded a boy to pose very uncomfortably and without his familiar spectacles. We hardly recognised him.

Constraining factors

The production of a constant volume of news to inhabit regular and fixed times and spaces inevitably places constraints and pressures on journalists. Although it is not recommended that much time is spent on this activity with young children, it is possible to examine how different newspapers each consistently apportion space and how this in turn might enhance the likelihood of particular subject matter being produced. It has been suggested[11] that because newspapers have sports commentators, foreign correspondents, crime reporters and so on their staff, this further commits the paper to a regular mixture of this news. Television and radio news broadcasts also operate under similar obligations. Here again the children can be asked to notice how television news is introduced by a title sequence (which, incidentally, can be analysed in the same way as an advertisement), how it occupies its apportioned time in the schedules and proceeds in a predictable, tightly structured and formal manner to deliver first the headlines and then the other news in descending order of importance, and how a programme often finishes with a light-hearted or sporting story.

Although such matters are noteworthy, primary children rarely show much interest in exercises like this. It is much more valuable to allow them to experience one of these constraints. An effective and simple way of demonstrating how the availability of air time shapes the raw material of a news item is to ask them to work in pairs/small groups and write a radio report about a recent event at which they were all present, bearing in mind that the story must include all the salient facts as well as being entertaining enough to hold the audience's interest. After these stories have been completed and perhaps, if this is not too threatening, a selection of them read aloud, the students should be given stop watches and told that their story can be given just 30 seconds of air time and must be edited to fit this exactly. The children should now audio-tape, or read out, their edited reports on the understanding that any which are too short will mean 'silent' air time, which may cause listeners to change to another wave length, and any which are too long will be cut off before they are finished. When the reports have been heard it is profitable to ask the children whether they felt the edited accounts were as accurate and entertaining as the unedited versions.

The limitation of space on the page of a newspaper has an effect on literary style, so before simulating the production of news in this medium it is valuable to ask the children to examine some newspaper articles, notice the style of writing and afterwards write about something familiar as if it were copy intended for a newspaper. A literary topic may offer opportunities for this kind of media education and recently, whilst reading Allan Ahlberg's story *Woof* (a tale of a boy who transmogrifies into a dog) to a group of first- and second-year juniors, I asked the children to write up a particular episode from the story in this way. The story had to contain all of the facts and be dramatic but it could occupy only a few lines of newsprint. The following was written by one 8 year old.

Dog or Boy?

A ten year old boy is missing. Friend, Roy Ackerman went to his house this morning. The boy's name is Eric Banks. A woman is said to have seen a Norfolk Terrier writing 'Eric' in the dirt . . .

(Becky Read, age 8)

Each child in the class produced a similar piece of copy and when they were compared it became clear that the shortage of space (as well as the viewpoint) determined which elements of the story were accentuated.

Space available on a newspaper page may also cause a photograph to be cropped to fit and this can distort the meaning of the image. Moreover, it is worth mentioning that the latest computer technology for retouching photographs is now able to alter images both quickly and undetectably to the extent that if two elements in the picture are too far apart they can be moved together.[12]

Hold the front page!

Simulating the production of the front page of a newspaper allows the children to recognise how news values operate in the process of news production. The creation of the following simulation owes much to teaching packs which have been devised for secondary schools.[13] From experience I can say that it is adaptable for most upper juniors but this can be achieved only in the knowledge of their abilities and interests.

During the few days prior to the lesson select from the local and national newspapers half or dozen or so stories and write (or preferably type) these out in your own words. At least one of these ought to be in note form. Secondly, cut out a further three or four stories – some of which need to have pictures to accompany them and at least one of which should be a 'minor disaster' which occurred abroad. In addition to these items, devise some public relations copy; for example, write about a shop or garage which has a spectacular offer or has received a promotional visit from a television personality. Several advertisements and perhaps a cartoon can be selected and cut from the newspapers. Finally it is necessary to create a story which would be of great local interest and which has not yet been resolved. For example:

> Six year old Emily Jones has now been missing from her – [name of town] home for two days. Her mother, father and her brother Jo are so worried they have not been able to eat or sleep. The little girl was last seen playing with her friends in the park. One of her friends, Claire Patterson, remembers seeing a large blue car near the edge of the playing area and a man who was dressed in a grey track suit was seen talking to Emily. She was wearing a green dress, white socks and yellow shoes. The police have set up an enquiry and any one who has any information should contact them immediately as concern is growing for the child. All of the children in the – [name of town] area have been asked to report anything suspicious to their parents and teachers.

A resolution to this story is then written in the form of an item of Late News.

Late News
> Emily Jones, found safe and well, wandering by herself in local park, got lost whilst gathering flowers, very tired, hungry, dirty. Family overjoyed.

Throughout the selection of stories it is vital, of course, to remember that they should be easily understood by the children. They must be recent so that the activity feels like reality and the children should be able to empathise or identify with the people and issues in the stories. Although this appears to be a lot of preparation, no teaching pack can do this adequately and any extra effort on the teacher's part is reimbursed in full by the children's enthusiastic responses to the simulation and by the relatively sophisticated learning outcomes.

When the preparation is complete, all of the items must be copied enough times for each group. With the exception of the 'Late News' and about three of the other news items, these should be placed in an envelope. Divide the children into mixed-ability groups of about five or six and give them an envelope of stories, a large piece of paper or card which has been blocked out as a newspaper page and a worksheet of instructions similar to Worksheet 6 on the following page.

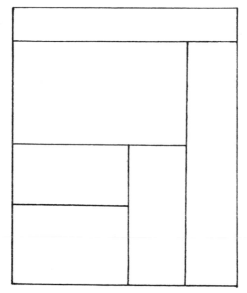

The simulation demands a vast range of social and linguistic skills – precis, expansion of a story, reading for meaning, lettering, discussion and decision making; more often than not, the children need at least a day to complete the task. At intervals during the day, distribute the remaining news items, leaving the 'Late News' until halfway through the afternoon. This always receives an emotional greeting!

Worksheet 6
Notes for the sub-editors

Today you are to compose the front page for a local newspaper. (The other pages have been composed earlier.)

The items in the envelope are those which have already been sorted as being suitable for the front page. However, during the day we expect several other stories to surface. These will be passed on to you as they arrive on the editor's desk. You will not have space to use all of the stories, so just leave the ones which you think will interest our readers. ADVICE: LEAVE THE MOST IMPORTANT STORIES TO THE LAST, THERE JUST MAY BE A LAST-MINUTE SCOOP WHICH WILL SELL MANY MORE COPIES OF THE PAPER.

1 *Items which have been given to you in note form will need to be written in good English if you decide to use them.*
2 *Some long items may need to be made shorter to fit into the space that is available on the page.*
3 *There must be at least one advertisement on the page. (This will help the paper sell at a profit.)*
4 *You may put a cartoon on the page if you think there should be one.*
5 *Choose a name for your paper.*

Having mentioned the skill of lettering which will be needed in the production, it is interesting to consider how the choice of this affects the overall appearance of the page. Graphic design is about making the product look right and lettering is an important feature of this. Print which has small lines at the ends of the strokes is referred to as 'serif' whereas that without lines is known as 'sanserif'. Usually serifed letters are easier to read, appear more stylish and enhance our aesthetic enjoyment, whereas sanserifed letters have a bold, blunt effect. Naturally newspapers, like advertisements, take advantage of these effects. Just take a look at the page of any newspaper – tabloid or broadsheet – to see how the medium of lettering transmits its own messages.

When all of the front pages are displayed, it is important to discuss with the children the reasons for their choices and positioning of the stories. There are many erudite analyses of the production of news which indicate the complexity of the process.[14] Nevertheless, many of the established news values will have been considered by the children in the course of the simulation and so it worth clarifying a few of the theoretical issues which we may wish to raise.

Most of the groups will probably have chosen at least one story about an elite person. News in general tends to centre around people rather than ideas – maybe because it is harder to envisage or to take a photograph of an idea. Negative stories always rank highly in the news, especially if they are dramatic. A story about the fall of an oak tree which has killed a workman will be chosen in preference to stories about the planting of saplings or the birth of a baby – unless of course those stories involve important personalities such as royalty. Bad news is usually dynamic; positive events are often slow. Ethnocentricity of news is frequently an issue which emerges from this exercise. The reader may be interested to see this example of writing which was produced by a fourth-year girl.

> When we had done the front page we had a discussion. We looked at how each group chose which story to have as the main story. Some people thought that a pet rabbit being savaged to death was more important than an Italian disaster. If it was a local paper I suppose that the pet rabbit story was more important.
>
> (Emma Coffey, age 11)

This was McLurg's Law in operation. McLurg was a duty editor of legendary reputation who is said to have established the rule of thumb which states that public interest diminishes with the degree of geographical remoteness of the event. So, for example, if one English person is involved in a disaster this news rates higher than a similar incident concerning fifty Europeans, but the latter would qualify as news in preference to a tragedy in a little-known African state which killed a hundred members of the indigenous population.[15]

Interviews

Interviewing is an important tool in the collection of information and opinion for any news medium, and it is a skill which should be isolated for practice before attempting to weave an interview into a simulated news production. It is vital that the questions posed should be of interest to the children. They must want to know the answers.

Some effective interviewing techniques were employed by my class of 8 year olds when they wrote stories for a specific audience. Although understanding about a sense of audience is considered in other sections of this book, it is worth a short digression to describe the role that interviewing played in enabling the children to elicit key information from their subjects.

The task was for each junior child to write a story for an infant who was to be interviewed in order to discover her/his personal tastes in literature. Through class dialogue it was decided that, because the interview was to be tape-recorded, the infants should be put at their ease. The junior should smile, maybe put an arm round the younger child, names should be exchanged, a cosy corner should be found and a friendly chat about family and pets should follow. Once this atmosphere was established the children proceeded to ask (not read) their questions. Back in school the junior pupils drafted their stories. These drafts were the subjects of sustained efforts and were the longest and best pieces of creative writing the children had composed to date. When they were ready, the stories were read to the infants. The critical feedback necessitated many changes but finally the stories were finished, bound and complemented with the infants' own charming illustrations.

Although the activity showed how interviewees are encouraged to give fruitful responses, it of course taught the children nothing about the constructed nature of television and radio interviews, so it was expedient to return to the audio tapes which the children made in order that these, which were somewhat disjointed, could be compared with a radio or television interview, which we can expect to have been edited to create the illusion that it was always as smooth as the finished product. Editing an audio cassette tape is technically difficult; however, we can still imagine and discuss how the interview could be improved by editing out unwanted material. It is also beneficial to explain a little of how the fluency of television interviews is manufactured. We can, for instance, point out that, when a film cuts, for a few seconds, to an interviewer's encouraging or serious face, this often indicates the presence of editing. Also it can be seen that the interviewee rarely or never authoritatively speaks directly to the camera but, when there is an emotive issue at stake, the sympathetic silences of the interviewer may encourage tears. When this happens the camera often cruelly closes in on those tears.

It is possible to explore a range of interviewing styles by simulating aggressive or supportive interviews.[16] For example, we can take a fairly innocuous subject such as holidays, and have the children construct interviews which suggest that the interviewee has been lazy or wrong in visiting a foreign country which is considered to be unfriendly to Britain. The same child can be treated to a sympathetic interview in which s/he is congratulated on his/her adventures. Interviews can be simulated where the interviewee refuses to communicate or persists in giving answers which are irrelevant to the issue being discussed.

The familiarity of the interviewer affects their credibility in adult eyes and this is no less so with children. After a group of fourth-year children had watched a television interview given by a well-known and loved comedian, I enquired if he were letting the children know the entire story of the African famine. The answer was immediate: 'Yes – he's going to find out for himself' (and by implication for us).

There is a great deal to discover by analysing interviews, and teachers who are interested to know a little more would do well to refer to Gillian Dyer's short article in *Screen Education*, even though this does concern older students.[17]

Radio news

A third simulation, which builds on some of the experiences previously suggested in this chapter, is the production of a short radio broadcast which uses several other news sources. This is then compared with an actual broadcast. Experience has shown me that it is realistic to attempt this only with fourth-year juniors or maybe with able third years who have had a fair amount of media education in the past.

Before going home on the evening before the simulation, the children should be told what they will be doing the next day and encouraged to read their own newspapers, watch a television news programme and listen to a radio broadcast the next morning before coming to school. The teacher needs to acquire as many of the day's papers as possible and these should be made available to the children.

Once again the class needs to work in balanced groups of five or six. It is their task to use the newspapers and their knowledge of the early morning broadcasts to create the lunch-time news. It is useful to stipulate that each group should conduct at least one interview. The work involved in editing and prioritising the stories is demanding but the pupils are usually highly motivated and cope with this better than would be anticipated. Before lunch the groups tape-record their news, which can be played after they have listened to a real radio version. (I have found the BBC's *The World at One* very suitable.) Afterwards there needs to be some time for evaluation and the groups should be asked to define their criteria for choosing or rejecting stories and say why they think their choice was similar to, or different from, the actual news.

As with the front-page simulation, many relatively sophisticated issues will have surfaced and the pupils should be helped to articulate what they have learnt and reflect on the values which caused them to select and prioritise the stories. Almost without exception the children begin their broadcasts with serious items which are later balanced by lighter ones, as they are aware that although news is serious it is also entertainment which needs to retain the listeners. Throughout the exercise it is necessary to choose events (which in this case have already been selected by other media) from a vast amount of information, and to create narratives and a structure which will bring order to what might otherwise be regarded as an unstable and uncontrollable world. It is now possible for the children to realise that their explanations of the events may have a reassuring effect on the listener.

The children should recognise that their overall news values must be compatible with the values of the perceived audience. So, for instance, when the offspring of an elite person died from an overdose of drugs, one fourth-year group saw that this fulfilled many of the criteria of a valuable news story. Another group in the same class felt that they could juxtapose the story with that of a hippy peace convoy which was causing problems in the south of England. In an interview with a traveller who disapproved of hard drugs, heroin was described as being 'the rich man's drug', and the children were fully aware that the positioning of this news item narrowed the range of possible interpretations of the phrase. They could understand that it was a very partial view of social reality which was making links between the events. The hippy convoy story was almost a 'non-event' on that particular day, for nothing intrinsically newsworthy had occurred. This illustrated that 'once something has hit the headlines and has been defined as "news" then it will continue to be defined as news for some time, even if the amplitude is drastically reduced'.[18]

News is not so unpredictable as we might believe. For their interview, one group of children decided to speak to England's football manager about his team's success in the World Cup. When asked, they told me that they had decided to ask him questions that they felt everyone would have liked to ask. In their role as broadcasters they had regarded themselves as representatives of the public image.

Many local radio stations employ education officers and it is worth contacting them to enquire whether it is feasible for the class to make a visit. If the children have experienced some of the simulations they become very excited when they actually watch the activities in a newsroom. We were particularly lucky as the education officer at our BBC regional station arranged for our group to observe the 6 o'clock news being read and afterwards go into the studio and talk to the people who worked there. The children were also taken into a studio which was not in use and allowed to record some news for themselves and then were taught how interviews are edited on reel-to-reel tapes using white pencil (China), razor blades and transparent sticky tape. Local newspapers can also be most generous and may give teachers valuable materials which illustrate the technical processes involved in creating a page of newsprint. Visits to the National Museum of Photography, Film and Television in Bradford and the Museum of the Moving Image in London are also efforts well rewarded.

Facing the camera

Although not many primary schools own a video recorder, if one can be borrowed from a teacher centre it is possible to develop the learning further by attempting a video simulation. Breakfast television news offers a somewhat different aspect of news production to simulate and there are already excellent instructions for doing this.[19] For those teachers unfamiliar with the technicalities of video work in the classroom I would recommend the pamphlet published by the Clwyd Media Studies Unit.[20]

Breakfast-time news differs in several ways from that broadcast at other times. Usually not much home news occurs overnight so yesterday's news is sometimes treated to a fresh slant. A little more foreign news may be chosen because good visuals can be acquired live by satellite from countries such as America where it is daylight. Generally, breakfast show hosts introduce the newscasters in a friendly fashion. Moreover, the frequency of the news 'slots' is tailored to a changing audience who are engaged in preparing for the day's work. Discussing how these factors may influence the viewers' responses to the subject matter, and comparing breakfast-time news with the mid-evening news broadcasts, can be illuminating.

Obviously the children enjoy using a video camera and it is worthwhile, but there are caveats. I have found that technical difficulties often disturb the flow of the simulation, and although it is exciting it does not feel 'real'. If one is not careful the filming tends to degenerate into an exercise which is simply normalising and emulating media conventions without much critical awareness. Moreover, the reflective discussion which follows is likely to focus on technical matters. Of course the range of incidental learning is enormous – everything from the artistic work of creating the title sequence to learning how to rectify the faulty wiring in a plug. Also it is possible to explore some of the visual techniques which operate as mediating filters and stand between the audience and the real world. For example, the children can notice that the news reader faces the camera and that s/he mostly is shown in close up.

Once the pupils have become familiar with the codes and conventions of news broadcasts, maybe a more effective and iconoclastic use of a video camera is to allow them to create a programme which breaks as many rules as possible. Trivial news can precede the serious, the newscaster can be shown without a desk and wearing outrageous clothes, there can be a total absence of negative items, and so on. In this case it does not matter whether the filming is technically perfect or not, but by doing this the children will interrupt the flow of realism and become aware that what masquerades as actuality is in fact a constructed media artefact.

CONCLUSION

The activities in this chapter do not pretend to be definitive or prescriptive blueprints for teaching about the news. Rather they are a medley of suggestions which could be instrumental in creating an open, questioning forum which is conducive to critical thought on behalf of both teacher and pupils. The fundamental intention is to create an atmosphere which fosters an enjoyment of learning together to appreciate the complexities of the news packaging process.

Chapter 4

Some approaches to teaching about advertising

The advertisement is one of the most difficult of modern literary forms. The problems presented by the sonnet are child's play compared with the problems of the advertisement.[1]

WHY CONCERN OURSELVES WITH MERE COMMERCIALS?

It was after Umberto Eco, the distinguished Italian writer, had explained to his very small daughter that the advertisement she had been credulously watching was not strictly true that he discovered 'If you want to use television for teaching somebody something, you first have to teach somebody how to use television';[2] for now this child's newly acquired suspicion of commercial messages was generalised to the weather forecast and, presumably, to the rest of the television's output. We can hardly blame her because television commercials are often similar to the actual programmes and, out of all media products, the advertisement has perhaps the most beguiling quality by virtue of its economic necessity to succeed. Its aim is to change our behaviour, but before it can achieve this it has, initially, to buttonhole our attention and then in about 30 seconds – if it is a television commercial, perhaps less if it is a poster – convince us that our future will be transformed by the purchase of this one product rather than any other.

Primary children watch a great deal of television and therefore advertising in this medium probably affects them more than any other single form of publicity. As far back as 1977 the Annan Report suggested that 'there should be a period set aside when children could watch programmes made for them on ITV without their being interrupted or flanked by advertisments';[3] however, this recommendation has been ignored. Clearly young people are not totally duped by everything they see in commercials, but they do watch and enjoy them and sometimes presumably buy, or put pressure on their parents to buy, some of the merchandise. Television advertisements are often fun as well as being technically and artistically excellent but, because advertising encapsulates our consumer culture in its most competitive and successful form, to me, as a primary school teacher, it seems sensible to begin educating the pupils, early in their lives, to be wise consumers. The National Curriculum document *English for ages 5–16* supports the view that children should be critically aware by including in the detailed provisions for pupils working towards level 5 of Attainment Target 2 (Reading) the following statement: 'They [the children] should be shown how to distinguish between fact and opinion in a variety of texts including newspapers, magazines and advertisements.' (§16:29)[4]

It has been estimated that, on average, young people watch about 350,000 advertisements before they are 18,[5] and, because many commercials have children as part of their target market, it is presumed that they intend to have a behavioural effect on them. This presumption is confirmed when we scan the pages of advertising and marketing journals such as *Admap*. A recent article presented

> some of the key facts and figures about school age children – their present and future numbers, their income and expendi-

ture patterns (and their influence on family expenditure), how they spend their leisure time and how they use the media, and the things they worry about.[6]

In the course of doing this it divided the children into social class groups and suggested that, because their spending power totalled about £2 million, 'No longer should manufacturers in many fields be content to know just the opinions of the adult purchaser; they should know also the images of their brands among the child consumers and purchasers of tomorrow'.

Even very young children can be encouraged to explore the potential influence of advertising and how it may shape their perceptions of the real world and their sense of social identity. Such learning should be valuable from a democratic viewpoint. Additionally the topic offers the primary school some highly motivating, cross-curricular activities which comply with many of the requirements of the National Curriculum.

Empirical studies have produced evidence of the consequences of commercials for such items as food, toys and medical products; of how stereotypes are perpetuated or modified; of how the volume and repetition of advertisements alter children's opinions of products. Attempts have also been made to show at what age children can differentiate between publicity and the actual programmes.[7] Although the majority of this kind of 'effects' research does not directly concern the approach to teaching about advertising described in this book, it should not be dismissed entirely. Instead, a knowledge of the empirical data can help us decide which aspects of advertising may be approached successfully and at what age.

Children can enjoy discovering how advertising determines both the structure and the content of the media, and how private companies influence such aspects of our culture as sport and the arts and to some extent information services. For instance, in the UK, the IBA's recent relaxation of sponsorship rules has allowed the PowerGen logo to appear on the weather forecast at the cost of £2 million a year. (Regional forecasts have local sponsors.) The children may be interested to know that for this advertising to be effective the company needs to be in a position to demand editorial influence – for example in the choice of the presenter.[8] Young people can also begin to understand that newspapers cannot be sold at affordable prices without the support of advertising revenue and that those newspapers which are unable to attract the necessary affluent, or large, readership fail to sell space to advertisers and therefore cease to be printed. Generally, television companies do not feel they can afford, for example, to show sports which have low audience ratings because, in the case of Independent Television, the advertisers will not buy space around the programmes. Consequently if these sports have a low television profile they will not attract the sponsorship funds which would promote their popularity.

In my experience most primary school pupils have, at best, only a vague notion of how commercial television is funded but arguably they should understand that many popular Independent Television programmes can survive only if they are able to deliver a suitable audience which can be sold to the advertisers. Although it is a highly complex issue – especially when we know that programmes on Channel 4 are often manifestly at odds with commercial ethics and that schools broadcasts have no advertisements – the general content of programmes shown on Independent Television is usually basically compatible with the values expressed in their commercial breaks. How many breweries would buy the commercial space during a programme which dealt with the deaths, injuries and misery caused through drinking and driving? This is a somewhat blatant example, but it has been suggested that frequently a commercial 'interacts through its styles with the kinds of drama – one might also say, the kinds of human simulation – which are common in "programme" material'.[9] Whether we are in agreement with this opinion or not, with the imminence of deregulation and the burgeoning of the new technologies, commercial interests will probably intensify and become an increasingly important determinant of media output.

Furthermore, in our society, the marketing of consumer products is not limited to overt advertisements. It has long been recognised by major companies such as Shell petrol or Pears soap that a powerful selling strategy is to forge associations between the product and the values of education, high culture or the beauties of the countryside. This is corporate advertising rather than product advertising. When Shell flatters the British public by calling us a 'nation of inventors' we experience a warm glow and so we are disposed to feel similarly towards the product. Because publicity is an inextricable component in our culture, children can be encouraged to explore how media content is inseparable from it. Often advertising emulates both the practices and products of the media in an attempt to woo consumers and gain credibility. For example, the mask of the 'Thundercats' commercial allows it to assume the persona of a 20 minute children's action-adventure programme. Moreover, and less attractively, the population is constantly subjected to intrusive marketing ploys such as direct mailing and telephone advertisements as well as to the subtle persuasions of press releases, product placement, public relations campaigns and other camouflaged marketing strategies which are frequently deceptively natural and often pass unnoticed. It has been suggested that for 'most of the time consumerism is engaged in persuading us to buy things we can do without, in re-defining luxury as necessity',[10] so an understanding of how publicity operates could be considered to be useful knowledge for all citizens.

Before suggesting some ideas for classroom approaches to learning about advertising, it is important to stress that the intention is to place the children on the inside of the processes of mediation and allow them to experience some of the problems which advertisers encounter. The pupils are then in a position to reflect on these experiences and evaluate how advertising influences their own codes of social values as well as learning to appreciate the advertisers' considerable skill. It is necessary therefore that, as teachers, we facilitate reflective learning by encouraging the children to talk freely and listen to the opinions of their peers. Although the suggestions for practical activities are presented in what I hope is a fairly coherent sequence, it is not envisaged that they will be followed in any prescriptive way. Whilst continuity is as desirable for media education as it is for any other area of the curriculum, it is clear that some of the exercises are more suited to younger or older children; moreover, most of the understanding gained at the primary stage of the child's cognitive development will need to be deepened in the future. As with all of the other ideas suggested in this book, the activities will require modification to match the needs, interests and capabilities of individual classes as well as changes in media practices. It should be borne in mind that all media education issues are interrelated and advertising is no exception. Therefore, because commercial influences permeate the mass media, suggestions for classroom activities involving advertising are not restricted to this section of the book. For instance, Chapter 5 on 'Representations of Reality' also offers practical ways of exploring how advertising exploits the deliberate use of stereotypes to sell products.

PRACTICAL APPROACHES

Introduction

Although much has been written about children's comprehension of advertisements, generally it is unwise to make assumptions about what is really understood. The first task is to encourage pupils to talk about advertising and what it means to them. If a camera is available and the school environment suitable, it is worth taking the class for a short walk around the immediate catchment area and have them photograph every advertisement they can find. Another easy way to initiate a dialogue is to video a collection of about a dozen television commercials, play the tape to the class and then ask the children to work in pairs or small groups – or as a class if this is more appropriate – to consider elementary questions such as those in Worksheet 7. (N.B. If the LEA has paid the required fee, the copyright rules allow the use of broadcast material in schools.)

Worksheet 7

1 *What are the purposes of these advertisements?*
2 *How do they try to persuade us to spend our money?*
3 *Do you think they will be successful?*
4 *Are their claims entirely truthful?*
5 *Make a list of the special tricks the advertisements use.*
6 *At what time of day would these advertisements have been shown?*

At this stage of the learning it is important that the teacher offers no judgements or information on the subject, as this would prejudice the direction of the dialogue. Naturally, the kinds of questions we ask depend on the age and ability of the pupils, but it is essential to listen to the children's responses as the range of understanding is usually as wide as it is surprising. For example, Mark, an 11-year-old boy in my class, did not realise that commercials were shown only on Channels 3 and 4 and yet he was an avid television viewer and by no means unintelligent. On the other hand, Alan, also 11, predicted that washing powder would be advertised during *Let's Pretend* (a programme for very young viewers) because he believed the manufacturers would be aware of the fact that mothers would be sitting watching the programme with their children and he said 'The mothers'll be the ones who will buy this sort of stuff'.

As with all media education, learning about advertising must be in response to the children's own experiences, pleasures and understanding, and the teaching must take its direction from what the pupils already know and what they need to understand about commercials in order to enable them to develop their critical faculties. Advertising is a highly sophisticated industry and the first time we introduce the topic into our curriculum we realise how little we know. Nevertheless, this should not deter our efforts. It is not necessary to be experts in this field of study any more than we need to be physicists to teach about 'forces' in primary school science. Instead we can enjoy searching for further information and understanding alongside the children.

Brand loyalty and the weekly shopping list

An effective method of helping children to understand why advertising exists in our society is to ask them to work in pairs, or in small groups, to devise a family's weekly shopping list (omitting any brand names of the provisions). When this is completed, have them place a tick by every itemised product which they have seen advertised. Most of the items will be awarded a tick. Now invite the pupils to name the possible brands of each of the items. The lists for common purchases like soap powder or margarine are long and as there is very little real difference between the brands it is necessary for the manufacturers to create illusory differences so as to engender 'brand loyalty'. One way of explaining this is to try the margarine test.

Can you tell margarine from margarine? – an experiment

Margarine is a product which most children consume, so ask them which brand they like best and why. In my experience the boys and girls are very definite about their answers and some are in the habit of refusing to eat bread which has been spread with the 'wrong' brand. This response is in keeping with the research, which has found that children develop brand loyalties in their early years.[11] When the favourite brands of the pupils have been identified, acquire about three of these and spread enough small pieces of bread to allow each child in the class to sample all three brands. However, keep the name of each brand secret (I usually use different coloured plates so that I know which brand is which) and as the children sample the margarine they need to be blindfolded because the colour of the product is usually a clue. The test must be kept scientifically fair by controlling the variables. Very rarely are the pupils able to identify the brand, although some do guess correctly. If the theme of advertising is being used as a cross-curricular topic, this lesson provides a meaningful introduction to the mathematical study of probability and chance.

Every advert tells a story

A simple method of exploring the advertisement's reliance on narrative to draw the consumer into an intellectual relationship with the commercial message it wishes to communicate is to tease out the stories told by the still pictures of magazine advertisements. First collect a wide selection of suitable ones. As a general rule these depict people engaged in mundane activities such as home care, eating out, relaxing, shopping, travelling and so forth. Begin by asking the children to work in pairs or small groups to study the picture in detail. I have found that the workcard in Worksheet 8 is an aid to discussion. (If you can find enough of the same advertisement it is possible to have a whole class work in pairs to analyse it. The comparison of the stories afterwards is a fascinating activity.)

Worksheet 8

1 *Look very carefully at this advertisement, talk about it with your friends and try to discover the story it is trying to tell.*
2 *It will help if you think about the following questions. If your picture shows people, what are they like: old or young, plain or beautiful, healthy or unhealthy? Say why you think this is so. How are the men and women, boys and girls shown? Who is the main character in the story? What have the people been doing before the picture was taken? What will they be doing next? Who took the photograph and why?*
3 *Who is supposed to buy the product which is being advertised? How can you tell?*
4 *Do pictures tell stories quicker than words or is it the other way round? Try to give reasons for your answer.*
5 *Write your version of the story. Either work by yourself or with your friend. If you work separately compare your stories afterwards.*

Usually the children find the task quite demanding and have to concentrate, but this itself is worthwhile and much of the writing is often highly perceptive. For example, this short story was produced by a 10-year-old boy after he had spent time examining an advertisement for Stork margarine which compared a sepia photograph of an angler and his child companion who were both dressed in old-fashioned clothes with a coloured photograph of a similar but more modern scene.

Give them back the taste of real home-baking.

An unmistakable taste. An extra bit of care. That's why real home-baking has always been so special. And that's why a packet of Stork has always been the proper margarine to use.

Well now we've made Stork even easier for you to cream. Easier to give them back the taste of real home-baking.

For a free recipe booklet featuring the best of traditional home-baking write to The Stork Cookery Service. Van den Berghs, Sussex House. Burgess Hill, Sussex.

New Stork Packet for real home-baking. It's only proper.

In 1957 a man and his son went fishing. At lunch time they opened their hamper to find Stork margarine. Thirty years later the same boy (who was now older) came fishing with his daughter. Nothing had changed with their equptment [*sic*]. When it came time for lunch they opened their hamper and the man was relieved to find Stork margarine with just the same taste as it was in his childhood. Nothing had changed over the years except the 'Stork' packaging.

(David Mountford, age 10)

Advertisements often masquerade as real stories, demonstrating the necessity for the advertiser to buy the reader with the entertainment of a narrative. It is now possible to compare this narrative technique with that of television commercials, many of which emulate the content of the programme material. For instance, there are series of advertisements for coffee and banks whose stories progress like romantic themes from a soap opera, and at the time of writing the Tesco 'chicken' commercials are similar to instalments of a comedy series.

Taking advertisements apart instead of taking them for granted

In whichever way one chooses to introduce a topic on advertising to a primary school class, it soon becomes apparent that the children love advertisements in the same way that they love television. This is not surprising considering that commercials are so much more expensive than the surrounding programmes and 'contain the concentrated entertaining and informative qualities which are spread out more thinly in the nonadvertising program content'.[12] The pupils are usually keen to tell you their current favourite advertisements and it is a good plan to video these in order to examine in detail some of their culturally shared references.

A short time ago my class of 10 and 11 year olds chose a Coca-Cola commercial to study. As suggested in the previous section, advertisements are similar to television programmes in that they usually adopt a narrative structure, so I proposed that we should begin by looking for the storyline. After viewing the advertisement we all realised that it was not just one 30 second story but rather a mosaic of about twenty tiny narratives. Using the video pause button, the children selected several of these

Coca-Cola stories to analyse. For example, they studied the image of two happy infants whose harmonious existence was disrupted by the breeze snatching out of their reach the red balloon with which they were playing. However, a new harmony was rapidly restored by the children's being given a drink of Coca-Cola. Methodically we played through the video tape and examined the remaining stories, all of whose miniature crises were resolved by the introduction of a drink of Coca-Cola. The product became the hero of the stories – always there to save the day.

We spent about an hour studying this advertisement, no one was bored, and it was not long before it became apparent that it was crammed with visual shorthand, codes and signs which enabled us, rapidly and effortlessly, to read the whole image. Each of the images was actually 'loaded with multiple meanings going far beyond what it seemed actually to say',[13] and we were being invited to identify with the images in a way that would make us reject our own values if we rejected the product. In fact to have criticised the advertisement would have been to criticise our culture. In subtle ways, the advertisement capitalised on our unconscious fears, and possibly our social inadequacies, which were to be dispelled by our acquiring the product. The implied message seemed to be that the people who drink Coca-Cola are unlikely to be rejected by society; on the contrary, they are the confident, happy, beautiful people and yet, like ourselves, they are engaged in normal everyday activities. If we drink Coca-Cola we too can be the beautiful people. By now we could all see that the advertisement was implying that it would be abnormal not to want the product.

Learning such as this extended the pupils' understanding of themselves as members of a particular culture and they understood that the commercial was communicating in such a manner that allowed the product to become a natural and integral component in our system of cultural values.[14] In this instance Coca-Cola was a panacea for emotional conflicts and, by taking the advertisement apart as we did, the children had explored how an advertisement can convey concentrated meanings by a few very powerful, evocative images whose signs and cultural codes are instantly understood.

Whatever we think about the products advertised, the commercial art must surely be admired and enjoyed, and the signs and codes of many commercials are a particularly rich source for studying how television transmits its meanings. Although children generally realise that the contents of advertisements are often wild exaggerations of actuality, frequently they still may not question many of the cultural details and representations. (They realise that using a certain bath oil will not conjure up a handsome male outside the window; however, they may take it for granted that this is every woman's wish.) Also it is worth remembering that in many commercials it is considered expedient that consumers are able to recognise their aspirant life styles and identify with the characters promoting the products.

It is very easy to find current television commercials which can be analysed in the way my class studied the Coca-Cola advertisement. The children are sometimes very sensitive to details and enjoy writing about them. The following is an extract from one pupil's analysis of a pipe tobacco advertisement.

> I did an advertisement on Condor tobacco. I chose that particular advert because it was funny and cleverly done. It starts with a man sitting peacefully beside a pond, in a park, smoking a pipe with Condor tobacco in it. The peace is broken when two teenadged [sic] boys come and start playing with their remote control boat, and they make a lot of racket. The man has a remote control submarine which shot the boat, and he is left to smoke his pipe in peace. I didn't see why it shouldn't be girls playing with a remote control boat. The boys in the advert didn't treat the ducks very nicely either. They just showed off to each other by chasing the ducks with their boat and started making quacking sounds at them. The advert sort of hinted that their product was the best by making the man insist on having perfect silents [sic] and the best atmosphere he could find to smoke his Condor tobacco in. Because he thought it deserved 'only the best'. That advert and the adverts with it were all on family viewing time, six o'clock on Sunday evening. They had an advert on for every member of the family. I think that that tobacco is more likely to sell than another *different* advert I saw. Because in the other advert it sounded more like a drug, and I think most people would prefer to pretend that tobacco isn't a drug.
>
> (Abaigael Offord, age 10)

This girl was aware of the narrative structure, the all-important connotations as well as the context in which the advertisement was shown. She and her peers were beginning to decode and explore some of the taken-for-granted values that underlie many of their everyday experiences of publicity which reinforce the culture and consumer ideology of our society.

A further way of developing the children's awareness of how the various sorts of commercial messages operate is to show a selection of advertisements with the sound turned down or alternatively to play just the sound tracks. This allows the pupils to separate visual evidence from music and verbal commentary. When a tape has been playing for a few seconds, press the pause button and ask the children to predict which type of product is about to be advertised and who the target market is to be.

Advertisements undoubtedly contain some of the most rich televisual imagery as they are designed to be watched repeatedly with enjoyment. It is important not to destroy this pleasure for the children by approaching the topic in a hostile manner. Rather the intention should be to alert their awareness so as to allow them to be critically questioning whilst at the same time appreciating the commercial art of the advertiser. A topic on advertising should always be a celebration of the art not a protection against it. In any case, in my experience, the children's enthusiastic pleasure in sharing their opinions about their favourite advertisements and their enjoyment of the work in general will always prevent the topic degenerating into an inoculative programme.

The technical events test

Having looked at the cultural messages which help to sell products it is worth exploring some of the televisual techniques which commercials exploit. In his book, *Four Arguments for the Elimination of Television*, Jerry Mander quite rightly points out that 'each time you are about to relax your attention, another "technical event" keeps you attached'.[15] Although we may not agree with the general argument of Mander's book, this particular piece of information has proved most useful in the classroom. By the term 'technical events' he means all of those essential techniques which distinguish television from reality, for example, the ability of the camera to zoom, pan, change scene or angle, for the screen to split, for words to appear as if by magic, and so on. He suggests that if we try a 'Technical Events Test' we discover that,

> on average, a thirty second commercial will have from ten to fifteen technical events. There is almost never a six second period without a technical event. What's more the technical events in advertising have much more dimension than those in the programming.

That is to say, they are technically more spectacular and varied.

Carrying out such a test in the classroom is great fun and very easy to do. Using a stop watch to check for accuracy, watch three 30 second commercials and three 30 second samples of random television and ask the children to count and tally the technical events. My own class performed the exercise a second time when they were at home, watching television, in the evening. When they converted their data into graphs it became obvious that Mander was correct. The mathematics which results from this exercise can range from simple block graphs representing an individual viewer's observations, to complex graphs comparing the various statistics. Although I have no evidence to support the notion, it has been suggested that some pupils could find this activity difficult. The argument is that

> Visual material is normally processed more or less unconsciously by the right side of the brain; the activity of counting forces the left side of the brain, with its more linear critical faculties, to remain involved. Television and film tend to be perceived by students as seamless extensions of reality; this exercise makes the seams visible. (Some students will, in fact, find this exercise difficult to complete: half-way through, these students are swept away by the images, and the left side of their brain goes back to sleep.)[16]

Because television poses as a 'window on the world' we often react to it as we do towards reality. We do not expect this 'reality' to be constructed and therefore any questioning appears to be redundant. Yet television images are carefully selected, and only packaged as reality. Unpacking an advertisement's tight structure lends itself to an understanding of television's methods of construction. The children can explore how the viewer's attention is retained by technical events, how truth can be refracted through exaggeration and how images which are shown for a few seconds can conjure up complex narratives. All of these strategies are able to be understood by young children, who can begin to gain insights into how television manufactures its own brand of reality.

Packaging the product

It is often appropriate to study in detail particular signs and codes which advertisers use to communicate their messages. Once again, examining the marketing of a commodity such as margarine may provide an ideal example. Each child can bring to school an empty margarine tub and, either in groups or as a class, it is possible to discuss how the container markets the product. When my class did this we discovered that the predominant colours used were green and gold and the children suggested that these were probably chosen because butter is golden and cows eat grass. Some brand names next came under scrutiny and it was decided that St Ivel sounded very much like St Ives in Cornwall, which conjured up holiday visions of golden sunshine, clear skies and lush green meadows; on the other hand the brand name Vitalite suggested health, fitness and vigour.

The children were learning that colours have cultural significance and that names can initiate a chain of connotations. To emphasise this further, I asked the pupils to suggest some colours which they felt were unsuitable for promoting the sale of margarine. No one had seen a black or grey margarine tub, for it seems that these colours have inappropriate associations. The class could understand that colours are a sign system which transmits powerful predetermined messages. The children can proceed to design their own margarine tub 'advertisements' by carefully measuring the shape of an existing container, cutting a piece of paper to the correct size to cover it and designing a package which creates a brand image. (This is a perfect exercise for design and technology and one from which the children may progress to design suitable packagings for a variety of products – fragile items, heavy goods, and so on.) Some pupils attempted to be more honest than the original margarine label by putting the additives in the same lettering as the healthier ingredients, whilst others made the brand names unattractive. However, many pupils simply designed a carton label which would sell the margarine.

A similar exercise is to have the children analyse and design a label for a can of soup. Firstly, they can examine the labels they bring from home to see where the brand name, the bar code, the ingredients and so on are placed and how the label contrives to attract the shopper's attention. Secondly, they can notice how the apparently innocent images on the label are able not simply to say how superior or economical the product is but also to imply for whom the soup is intended.

It soon becomes clear that the images are communicating, not just on their face value but also at a second connotative level. It is unnecessary in the junior school to do any more than discuss this notion: 'the important thing is to make the invisible, visible, so that each mass media consumer is in a position to evaluate for him or herself.'[17] By making visible this deeper level of communication, which operates at the level of accepted cultural codes, the children begin to see how patterns of meaning emerge. They can now set about designing their own labels but perhaps, this time, with a target market in mind. Some may decide to aim at children, others at the hungry worker, while others may attempt to attract the connoisseur. It is fun to encourage each child to use his or her family name as the brand name because they usually derive an enormous amount of pleasure and success from the exercise of selling their own name. At whatever level the children operate, they no longer take packagings for granted; instead they actively search for significant details, realising that these are non-accidental, and they can experience how it is possible that reality can be defined for them by commercial interests.

Looking at logos

Logotypes such as those employed by institutions and companies typify how effective publicity needs to inform both rapidly and memorably. After a class discussion of what logos are and how they operate, at home the children can make a collection from magazines, newspapers and so forth and these can be brought into school. Often the collections are enormous. The pupils, their parents and I have been overwhelmed by the ubiquity of the logo. One boy's mother expressed her amazement both at the sheer amount that she and her son had discovered and also at how much she herself had assimilated about the commercial enterprises without being aware of doing so. Asking the children to perform activities like this at home often absorbs the whole family and offers teachers a good basis on which to discuss the value of media education when we meet the parents.

The analyses of the logos can be as detailed or as simple as you like and it really depends on the age and ability of the children, but the following is how my own class of 10 year olds analysed three logos. These were British Rail, Nottinghamshire County Council, and the book token. The British Rail logo tersely informed the pupils that trains travel as fast as arrows in both directions along parallel lines, whereas the simple 'N' of Nottinghamshire which surrounds the Major Oak indicated that our county protects and is proud of its inheritance and the legend of Robin Hood. However, it was the book-token logo that inspired some of the most ingenious ideas. The children saw the dove's wings forming the cosy pages of a book where peace could be found whilst at the same time they could freely indulge in flights of fancy and enjoy a bird's eye view of the world. After deconstructing logos the pupils can set about designing some for themselves.

Throughout a lesson such as this, I believe it is not so much what the children discover about specific logotypes which is important but rather the fact that they are involved in searching beneath the superficial level of communication to find the more complex messages of these economical symbols which are designed to be effective marketing strategies. An investigative frame of mind is essential for this exercise, which involves both the children and the teacher in concentrating their attention on details which are often missed because they appear to be so artless and simple and yet when examined in the light of their cultural meanings are revealed to be both persuasive and complex. As a result of such activities the pupils begin to understand how colours, images and slogans are loaded with covert meanings which can be communicated both instantly and effortlessly.

Because advertisements need to sell consumer products they tend to reflect the ideological assumptions of our consumer culture. However, it can be argued that consumerism merely creates a pseudo-world in which we appear to become what we consume. Although it may be something of an exaggeration, it has been claimed that advertising helps to perpetuate the myth of freedom to the extent that 'the choice of what one eats (wears or drives) takes the place of significant political choice' and that 'publicity helps mask and compensate for all that is undemocratic in society'.[18] The argument follows that because we are 'free' to consume these products we are also persuaded to believe that it is in our power to influence our social position, whereas in reality these circumstances are largely determined, not by ourselves, but by economic power structures which are beyond our control. Consequently if we can enable children to demythologise advertisements and consider how commercial messages affect us all, our pupils ought to be in a better position to analyse the way that publicity could be influencing their values.

Advertising the unsellable

As it was suggested earlier on in this chapter, in our society, 'where a reasonably large part of its population lives above subsistence level, advertising is inevitable'.[19] It functions as an economic device for creating markets; manufacturers need to engender a desire for the product and then prove that the consumers need it. However, like the margarine advertisements, most commercials cannot tell the whole truth for it is 'precisely their function to improve on the deflating actuality'.[20] Nevertheless, some new products are ultimately both unpopular and impractical and consequently fail. Do you remember the Sinclair C5? It is fun to set the children the task of promoting the sale of an unpopular product – maybe a boring food such as cabbage or an undesirable object like a brown paper bag – or maybe the pupils could set a fashion trend in their school. The class can produce publicity posters, storyboards for television commercials, stickers and so on. Through doing this exercise it is possible to show that advertisers, by media saturation, are often able to convince the public that their products are desirable. The multi-million dollar success of the 'Teenage Mutant Hero Turtle' toys is an example of this.

Cigarette advertising and health education

The marketing of cigarettes has stretched the advertisers' skills
to the full. After all, what is a cigarette but dried leaves containing nicotine poison, wrapped up in a piece of paper? It is well
known that smoking is Britain's greatest health hazard, causing
50,000 premature deaths every year and damaging the well-
being of thousands more.[21] In addition to the government
health warning and the ban on television advertising there are
other restrictions on what cigarette manufacturers are allowed
to show. For example, no advertisement can present images
which are associated with glamour, manliness, wealth, success
or sporting prowess and no famous person is allowed to promote cigarettes. No commercial is permitted to feature anyone
smoking who appears to be under the age of 25 nor can they
imply that consuming cigarettes induces relaxation. Yet £100
million each year is spent on cigarette advertising, public relations exercises and sponsorship by the tobacco companies.
They recognise that if children do not begin smoking before they
are fully adult then it is unlikely that they will start to do so.
Consequently their target markets are the young, women, current smokers, developing countries and the users of other
tobacco products.

Teaching about the advertising of tobacco does address a
serious health education issue and, although as teachers we
must avoid being too judgemental, as well as being careful not
to offend children whose parents smoke, maybe insightful connections can be made only in the light of relevant knowledge.
The intention is to educate the children about advertising
methods so that they can make informed decisions about
whether or not to heed the tobacco companies' messages.
Therefore initially it is a good idea to explain the current facts to
the children and ask them to spot instances of where the publicity is questionable. For example, at present, a government
health warning must be included on all posters which are more
than 260cm^2 (40 square inches). Most small shops have these on
their doors or framing the shop window. Ask the class to see
how many of their local shops' advertisements break or bend
the agreement. At the time of writing, television allows six
minutes in every hour for sponsorship – for example in a soccer
match. Invite the children to notice where the cigarette advertiser's board is placed during tennis matches. (It is usually next

to the umpire's desk. The excuse here is that the umpire is not an active participant in the game.) The 1986 Voluntary Agreement on Tobacco Advertising specified that no advertisements were to be allowed 'in close proximity to and clearly visible and identifiable from within buildings or boundaries of schools, places of education or playgrounds'. See how many posters the children can find which break this agreement. Television is not allowed to show anyone lighting a cigarette. Ask the pupils if they have seen this act during a snooker match.

An enjoyable art exercise is to parody the advertisers' skills. Suggest that the students collect as many cigarette advertisements as possible from magazines and then have them work in pairs, or small groups, to re-draw the advertisement but this time subtly altering the meaning. For example, a recent Benson and Hedges advertisement featured the letters B and H pegged on a washing-line. As far as one class of second-year juniors and their teacher could understand, this poster's meaning seemed to be that the woman's household work was completed, the clothes were hanging out to dry and it was time for a break and a Benson and Hedges cigarette. These 8 year-old children re-drew the poster but added the captions: 'Don't Hang Your Life on the Line', 'Clothes Wash, Lungs Don't'.

Once the pupils become interested they will probably notice the plethora of 'brand stretchers' which are produced by cigarette companies; that is to say, mugs, anoraks, sun-shields and so on which bear the name or colours of the brand of cigarettes. With older juniors it is worth asking them to look out for press items which muddle the issues and arguments and which represent non-smokers as fanatics or kill joys.

Because cigarette advertising needs to be oblique, it is satisfying to have the children deconstruct the advertisements so as to identify the selling strategies which are being employed. Junior pupils are usually quite capable of spotting associations, hidden levels of meaning and the visual puzzles which engage our minds and force us to interact with the advertisement. This is an engagement which usually results in a feeling of smugness when the puzzle has been solved.

The selling of cigarettes has not always been subject to the current heavy restrictions and it is worthwhile comparing contemporary advertisements with those of the past. Roland Marchand's book *Advertising the American Dream*,[22] which traces the development of advertising from 1920 to 1940, reproduces a selection of cigarette advertisements from this period which permitted completely different strategies. Around this time many cigarette companies attempted to persuade the public to smoke rather than to eat sweets; moreover, it was claimed that a process known as 'toasting' the tobacco protected the smoker's throat. Even twenty years ago the promotion of cigarettes was much less sophisticated than it is now and if advertisements from this period can be traced, the children can see how marketing strategies have needed to evolve.

Using a video camera to create a commercial

Although I would wish to argue that the use of a video camera is neither necessary nor always advantageous, if one is available it is worthwhile simulating the production of a television commercial. Afterwards we can help the pupils to examine their experiences, reflect upon the conventions which they employed and explore what determined their own creative processes. Because media education is quintessentially a critical practice we must be mindful that the pupils are not merely imitating or emulating the professionals, although during the process of the learning it will seem very much like this. Obviously any video work produced in schools is necessarily amateurish and the children can often be disappointed with their final commercial if it is compared with those which are shown on television.

If a video commercial is to be attempted, and it must be said that the girls and boys always derive a great deal of pleasure from the activity, it is worthwhile spending time considering the audience for which it is intended. The children may decide to create a commercial for breakfast television. For this they will need to know that *TV-am* is a nationwide broadcast supported entirely by advertising revenue. It is a good idea to watch the programme and monitor which advertisers buy the commercial time, how many commercial breaks are contained within one hour of viewing, the number of advertisements shown, and so on. Obviously it will depend on the age and ability of the class, but it may be a good idea to explain to them that these commercials are cheaper than the evening ones owing to the fact that they are buying a smaller audience. For example, a 30 second *TV-am* advertisement could cost £4,800 whereas the same commercial may cost £14,000 during prime time evening viewing[23]. (To find the current costs of advertisements it is possible to write to your local commercial television company and ask if you may receive their rate card.) On *TV-am*, 'feature advertising is available as never before, with advertisers encouraged to buy time next to specific slots in the programme relating to sport, farming, cooking'.[24] By watching the programme it will be discovered that the commercial breaks are shorter but more frequent, so advertisers have less competition for attention. It may be felt necessary to explain to the pupils that the original presenters had a close relationship with the advertisers. In a video aimed at the advertisers and shown a short while before *TV-am* began, Michael Parkinson informed them that the programme would deliver 'the most receptive audience any advertisers could ask for'.[25] Moreover, and most distastefully, the social class of the audience was described in demographic jargon. However, we have to face the fact that this *is* how advertisers view their audience and hiding it from children would be dishonest.

The class can watch a selection of *TV-am*'s commercials and decide which commodities are likely to be advertised at this time and notice the style of the commercials. Because the early morning is usually a busy period in the home the advertisers have to grab the attention of the audience; therefore soft music is not useful, and colour techniques cannot be relied upon as the programme is sometimes watched on a black and white 'second' set in the kitchen or the bedroom. At this time of the day the advertisements have to be direct and snappy. Sweets and newspapers, which are likely to be bought en route to work or school, and toothpaste, coffee, milk and cereals that are being consumed in the morning are all likely candidates. So for their own commercial the children may decide to produce advertisements for such items, which can then be placed near to appropriate features in the programme. It is sensible to plan a broad outline of what the actual programme will contain and in this way show 'media content and advertising as inextricably bound together'.[26]

Video cameras are not widely available in primary school; however, it is usually possible to use an audio cassette recorder to produce an advertisement for commercial radio. To some extent this is often more satisfactory, and the same processes of creation, reflection and deconstruction can be followed as for the video recording. Moreover, the children enjoy creating sound effects and generally exploiting the medium of radio.

Using 'free' newspapers

Clearly it is unrealistic to study advertising in isolation from other marketing strategies and at some stage it is essential that children are introduced to the notion of public relations and how PR, which largely depends on a lack of awareness for its potency, is able to be included in many media products. Maybe the most obvious form of marketing, which actually impersonates a media product, is the 'free' newspaper that arrives in most homes each week. A critical glance at any one of these publications reveals that the articles, if not blatant advertisements, are hooks for the advertisements which surround them (articles like this are known as 'puffs'), and so the journalism is almost totally usurped by publicity. To acquire cheap advertising space, companies create 'advertorials', that is to say advertising material, which poses as articles. The ordinary press usually shun this type of copy but the 'free' newspapers are littered with it.

Multiple copies of these newspapers are easy to obtain and they can be utilised in the classroom for many worthwhile investigations. Before using them with children it is profitable for the teacher to know a little about the history of these publications. The boom in their birthrate came in the early 1970s, perhaps because the provincial, paid-for newspapers were undergoing a financially difficult period and their existence was threatened. Technology in the printing industry had made it possible for newspapers to be produced more easily; consequently they could be managed with a minimal staff. Advertisers saw the 'free' paper as an effective way to reach local target markets. A paid-for newspaper consists of about 36 per cent editorial material and articles and employs maybe eighty members of staff, whereas a 'free' newspaper usually contains around 20–25 per cent editorial content plus articles and frequently employs one editor and one reporter. Recently a 'free' newspaper in Cheshire was operating with no editorial staff and simply gained its news from a news agency. In December 1986, 36 million copies of 'free' newspapers reached an audience of 73 per cent of all adults, whereas 23 million paid-for newspapers reached 53 per cent of all adults.

There are, however, a number of advantages to the proliferation of such publications. They provide cheap local coverage of events, therefore they are good for local democracy. To illustrate this point it is fun to have the children write some press releases describing seasonal events which could help to promote the good reputation of their school. These can be sent to the local 'free' newspapers and often they are published. Some 'free' papers have helped the paid-for newspapers in that they are produced by the same company in order to kill the competition for advertising revenue. In effect they subsidise the newspaper because the advertisements are placed in both the 'free' paper and the paid-for newspaper as a package deal.

On the other hand, frequently the 'free' press employs untrained journalists, whose lack of knowledge of legal matters prevents the reporting of court news. Consequently local crimes are often not reported. Also news items are sometimes simply rewritten from local newspapers and so news gathering becomes passive rather than active or investigative. Council affairs are rarely reported as this is not always in the interests of the publication, even though it is in the interests of democracy. Finally, 'free' newspapers prioritise the values of consumption.

Initially it may be a good plan to ask the children where they think the money comes from for the cost and the delivery of the paper. The answers usually range from 'local rates' to 'funding from central government'. After studying the content of the 'free' papers, the pupils will discover for themselves that ultimately the recipient pays for the paper by his or her positive response to the advertisements.

Having obtained enough copies of the same edition of the local 'free' newspaper, distribute these to the class, who can work in groups to analyse the contents. This work is most suited to the third- and fourth-year junior school children as the reading material is often quite difficult. The pupils will need guidance and I have found the material in Worksheet 9 helpful.

The incidental learning which arises from this activity can include mathematical estimation, scale, percentages and a wealth of purposeful language work.

Another approach to this activity is to provide each group of children with two copies of the paper. (This is so that each side of the page can be used.) Have them cut out all of the advertisements, advertorials and other marketing material and stick it

Worksheet 9

1 Make a graph to show the proportion of advertisements to articles.
2 Read the articles to see if they are really advertisements.
3 Compare the proportion of advertisements in this 'free' newspaper with the advertisements in ordinary papers.
4 How is it possible that this newspaper is free?
5 What kinds of advertisements are found in this 'free' newspaper?
6 Why do you think the editor of this 'free' paper picked these particular stories?
7 Who writes the articles in the 'free' newspaper?

onto a large piece of paper. Now ask the pupils to stick the rest, that is to say the bona fide copy, onto a second sheet of paper. If time is short the groups can do just one page each. In any case the results are certainly worth the effort.

It is apparent to the children that the vast majority of the copy in the newspaper issues from commercial sources or is written with the advertiser in mind. The pupils soon begin to understand how advertising acts as a determinant of the content of even the ordinary press. What is more, they begin to see how 'the close association of advertisements with particular features . . . actively distorts news values'.[27]

Moreover, it becomes clear that:

> Ads are *news*. What is wrong with them is that they are always *good* news. In order to balance off the effects and sell good news it is necessary to have a lot of bad news. *Real* news is *bad* news.[28]

Even the 'free' newspaper has to balance its advertisements with bad news; for example, stories of local vandals and other petty crime.

To support this assignment on how public relations and other marketing strategies operate in the 'free' newspapers, it is useful to alert the children to how even programmes like *Blue Peter*, *Jim'll Fix It* and *Wogan* are often vehicles for commercial messages in the form of information about records, books, exhibitions, films, concerts and so on. It is also worthwhile exploring how advertisements in newspapers and magazines are often juxtaposed with relevant articles. At the time of writing this chapter, the 'problem' page of the *TV Times* contained the following suggestion from Dr Miriam Stoppard:

> Oats in any form are good for you, not particularly porridge. And the magic ingredient is all that gluey sticky stuff. It's called soluble fibre and it works by binding to cholesterol in the intestine, preventing its absorption so the cholesterol never actually reaches the blood stream.

Facing this advice page is a whole-page colour advertisement for Kellogg's Common Sense Oat Bran Flakes, which claim to stop cholesterol aiming straight for the heart.[29]

Product placement

The realism of many popular television programmes and films is enhanced by the characters being surrounded by familiar household branded products. Obviously much of this is unavoidable unless fictional brand names are to be created in the way that *Coronation Street* created the brewery Newton and Ridley. However, the tantalising question remains: are these products chosen in a purely random fashion or do the manufacturers know that their products will star, for example, alongside the much-loved cast of a popular soap opera? Advertising is so expensive that a 30 second commercial at peak viewing time is worth a king's ransom, so imagine the joy and surprise of the manufacturers of Golden Wonder crisps when their goods are shown repeatedly in *EastEnders*. Can we believe that it is chance when leaflets drop through our door which offer 10 pence off a packet of Persil washpowder and which feature a picture from the title sequence of this same soap opera. Persil maybe were cashing in on a coincidence, but in any case the BBC rubric is that real products can be used to give a dramatic scene a tinge of reality so long as they are not gratuitous.[30]

In his book *Advertising: The Uneasy Persuasion*,[31] Michael Schudson describes how companies – notably Associated Film Productions – specialise in placing products in films; for example, the Nikon camera in *Hopscotch*, Wheaties in *Rocky III*, Coca-Cola in *Missing*. Moreover, undertakings were made that none of the products would be used by the bad guys. No doubt the readers of this chapter will be able to spot their own

examples. This is precisely what we can ask the children to do. At home, say for one week, whilst they are watching their normal television programmes the pupils can be asked to spot the secret ads, noting the programme and the time of transmission. When I asked my class of fourth years to do this the results were amazing and from the data collected it was possible to make some tentative generalisations. It was noticed that British soap operas featured more branded goods than any other genre. However, one child said:

> I was watching *Dallas* and I looked quite closely and I couldn't see any [branded goods]. That's probably because in America the big companies have enough time during the breaks to squeeze in an advert.

Whether her hypothesis was correct or not, this girl was able to question and compare how advertising was determining the content, in this case the realism, of the programme.

An advertising campaign

After learning some of the marketing techniques and the arts of commercial persuasion, the children usually enjoy the challenge of conducting a real advertising campaign. The first task is to identify something which your school would like to sell – it may be books from the school bookshop, snacks from the tuckshop, school dinners or tickets for a PTA outing. Our own school was having difficulty selling tickets for the 'St Valentine Disco' and, as the profits from the proceeds were needed to swell the school fund, a fourth-year class decided advertising could be the answer.

After conducting some research to discover how many children had already bought, or intended to buy, tickets, they converted their data into block graphs which identified the gaps in the market. The pupils then worked cooperatively in small groups to attack these gaps. They saturated the school with posters, heart-shaped badges, bookmarkers, mobiles and information and took every opportunity to sell their product. A dramatic sketch on the lines of a television advertisement was delivered to the classes which had few children intending to go, just before they left for home in the evening, and more sketches were presented in assembly. To prepare for each of these mini-plays the children can create a storyboard using photographs; under each photograph they can write the action and the dialogue. This activity proved to be a very useful vehicle for practising the use of direct speech.

It is not long before the students realise that advertising is an expensive business. Balloons, little confectioneries and so forth, which were to be given away as a promotion exercise, needed to be successful in selling more disco tickets or the school fund would be further out of pocket. Time was of the essence.

Throughout the campaign the children had to remember that adverts use narrative to wrap the product; they had to link the disco with attractive attributes – health, fitness, youth, excitement, vitality and so on – but they also needed to remember the legal code of advertising which stipulates that an advertisement must be honest.[32] The pupils were having to acquire a sense of audience; one group designed posters in the style of comics because they knew that this was a favourite reading matter of many boys and girls. Once the children felt that they were really part of an advertising campaign they worked with an enthusiasm which spread into playtimes and they laboured both before and after school hours.

Maybe the most effective learning takes place after the campaign is over. In our case the disco had been a real success: the money and the time spent had resulted in a high attendance and the pupils were able to record their statistics graphically. During the week the class had made a book charting the progress of the campaign and the marketing strategies. The children were now able to reflect on the process of their own learning and compare their problems and strategies with those of professional advertising agencies.

FOOTNOTE

During any teaching about advertising, it is important to consider not only how advertising determines the structure and content of media products, but also how such publicity effectively uses the language of the media in the art of persuasion. It could be argued that a class project on advertising is somewhat different from other media topics, because, whether we like it or not, commercial messages are designed solely to have a behavioural effect on the reader or viewer. However, throughout this chapter I have advocated what I hope will be interpreted as a positive and analytical approach to the subject, whilst at the same time reminding the reader of some of the hard facts which are fundamental to the advertising industry's work.

It is not a particularly comfortable thought but it is worth our bearing in mind that the Canadian writer Dallas Smythe accused schools of implicitly imparting 'submissiveness to authority' and consequently robbing media audiences of their critical freedom, which in turn allows them to be bought and 'produced as (audience) commodities'.[33] He saw the media as 'consciousness industries' which relentlessly pressurise people into the acceptance of the media's own values. Such a critical enslavement is an unattractive prospect. It is a limitation of the very freedom which, paradoxically, the advertiser would claim to sell. So, to help pupils develop their critical freedom, whether we agree with Smythe's theory or not, it is worth analysing how commercial messages operate. Activities which facilitate the sharing of opinions, pleasures and experiences of advertisements are likely to raise issues and open dialogues which may contribute to the child's ability to make more informed choices.

Chapter 5

Representations of reality

In order for televisual representations of the real to appear as 'real', to correspond apparently exactly, then they must be able to deny their own status as products. . . . It is this denial of a production process, posing as the 'obvious' and natural, which is a realistic mode of production.[1]

REALITY, REALISM, REPRESENTATIONS

In his book *Visible Fictions*,[2] John Ellis discusses the 1955 film *All That Heaven Allows*, which features a television salesman who describes his merchandise as 'All the company you want: drama, comedy, life's parade at your fingertips'; but, as Ellis explains, this parade is split into a variety of genres which emphasise some aspects of reality and ignore others completely. As we know, the media are not 'windows on the world' but rather carefully constructed representations. However, the illusion is such that we often experience media products as if they were reality because the skills of the producers facilitate the temporary suspension of our disbelief. Throughout our teaching we must remember that it is our aim to enhance the considerable pleasures which these experiences bring whilst at the same time opening up a dialogue on how media realism is achieved and how representations are constructed. I hope to show in this chapter how critical awareness and enjoyment are allies not enemies.

Modern literary theory offers us a multitude of definitions of the term 'realism'; in fact, perhaps we should talk about 'realisms'.[3] As Jane Root points out, children respond to a car crash in the *A Team* differently from the way they react to a motorway pile-up on the news because the conventions of these realisms are easily distinguishable.[4] The realistic effects of drama and documentary are sometimes interchangeable and necessitate the coining of media terms such as 'docudrama'; on the other hand, as with literature and plays such as those of Bertolt Brecht, the author of a television play may reveal the devices used so that the viewer is 'encouraged to reflect critically on the partial, particular ways they construct reality and so recognise how it might all have happened differently'.[5]

Academic discourse on realism is intriguing and even at primary level we cannot ignore textual constructions and conventions when teaching about media products such as soap opera. Realism inevitably transmits its own value systems and when we consider that it is from media evidence that most of us conceptualise Africa, the work of the police force, the social life in the east end of London, and so on – whether the information arises from documentary or dramatic sources – it is clear why we should examine how its ostensible authenticity is constructed. Although it is too abstract and nebulous a concept to be discussed directly at primary level, it can be approached in more concrete ways which are well within the children's frames of reference and will eventually contribute to an understanding of the notion of realism. Representations of ethnicity, age, gender and disability immediately spring to mind and, even though these are sometimes sensitive issues, with sympathetic handling they can be effectively considered in the primary classroom.

It is often argued that, although the media may contribute to the perpetuation of gender, racial and other stereotypical roles, it is also true that they did not create them. Gerbner called the relationship between the media and culture 'cultivation'; that is to say, the media help to maintain, propagate and adapt the culture's existing values.[6] Nevertheless the media can, to some extent, be considered to be socialising agencies and as such they contribute to the creation of our value systems and our understanding of society's expectations.

Bearing in mind that approximately 50 per cent of the population is female, that recent statistics indicate that 4.5 per cent is of a different ethnic origin and that about one in five people in the country is over 60,[7] it might seem reasonable to expect to find these categories of people represented on television in commensurate proportions. Even at the level of a numerical content analysis this is nowhere near the truth. Space does not permit my offering all of the detailed statistics but it is worth looking, very briefly, at the research into representations of one of these categories. Women comprise the largest category, so I have chosen this.

The ratio of men to women shown on television is 7:3,[8] and various researchers have found that between 70 and 85 per cent of the characters in children's programmes are male,[9] and moreover they are more dominant.[10] This statistical research was conducted a few years ago and the situation may have improved minimally, but there is still a dearth of good female role models and it is with good reason that this situation has been termed 'symbolic annihilation'.[11] It is noteworthy that some research into children's understanding of television and real life models has chosen to use just boys because of the greater range of male leading characters.[12] Kevin Durkin, in his book *Television, Sex Roles and Children*,[13] argued that, although television was only one factor in the child's understanding of sex roles, television was more likely to confirm than initiate perceptions, and Hodge and Tripp suggest that this 'incredible bias' in television's representation of gender during childhood 'must . . . contribute to a chauvinistic view of girls and women'.[14] During their research with over 600 primary aged children they found that 'Each boy talks twice as much as each girl, on average, though they certainly do not watch twice as much television and it can be doubted that they think twice as much.' In my own action research I attempted to discriminate positively towards the girls during discussion times but when the audio-tape recordings were transcribed I found that the children's contributions had followed roughly the same trends as those of Hodge and Tripp.[15]

It is in advertising that some of the most derogatory images of women appear. Anyone watching a sample of television commercials would never guess that about 11.1 million women (rather more than half of all women of work age) now have jobs outside the home. It is generally the case that women are sold commodities for their work of child care, domesticity and beautification,[16] so girls watching advertisements are generally presented with a restricted range of role models. Some research has even concluded that the styles of commercials targeted at girls are less active than those targeted at boys and therefore help to socialise girls into more passive roles.[17] However, to play devil's advocate for a moment, why should advertisers jeopardise the efficacy of their commercial messages? They do not claim to have any obligation to change social attitudes; their only responsibility is to change spending patterns. Because advertising is exorbitantly expensive, advertisers need to employ visual imagery which is rapidly assimilated and which consequently exploits stereotypical representations that often limit and undervalue the potential of women.

PRACTICAL APPROACHES

Comics and cultural values

Exploring the media's methods of representing the social world necessitates examining its use of stereotypical images. Although stereotyping is a socially unavoidable mechanism which we all use for ordering and making sense of a complex world, the media are often condemned for operating this form of cultural coding to the detriment of some social groups. The accumulation of images of unruly comprehensive school pupils or submissive housewives may assist the writers of situation comedies who need to create instantly recognisable characters for their 25 minute dramas, but it is an abuse which should be made visible. The cognitive processing of stereotypical representations is usually both automatic and rapid, but by devising activities which allow children to analyse the significant elements which combine to produce these images it is possible to establish that 'the stereotype is a myth or disguised explanation of the values that are held by significant numbers in our culture'.[18]

An easy and pleasurable introduction to this notion is to have the children discuss the characteristics of some well-known comic characters. The comic is one of the few common links between the teacher's popular culture and that of her pupils. Nostalgia certainly allows me to empathise with the child who listens for Thursday's flip of the letter box, heralding the arrival of The Beano and the promise of an escape into the world of Lord Snooty or the Bash Street Kids. We know that our favourite characters are not like real people but this does not stop our identifying with them. A cursory glance at copies of The Beano and The Dandy reveals their characterisations to be overwhelmingly imperialist and sex stereotyped. For instance, on the first page of The Dandy (4/3/89) there was an ethnocentric representation of a diminutive Japanese businessman; the second page portrayed a brash, obese, check-trousered, cap-wearing, camera-wielding American tourist with his wife Elmer; the third page showed a back-slapping 'Aussie' with a cork-trimmed hat and a pet kangaroo. The only black person to appear in the same week's edition of The Beano was a fuzzy-headed character from 'darkest Africa' who wore a grass skirt and carried a drum under his arm. Needless to say, there are proportionately far fewer positive female than male characters in both of these publications.

Had these damaging representations appeared in any other literature aimed at children they would have quite rightly incurred the censorship of all concerned with good educational and moral practice. Nevertheless, whatever our adult opinions may be, traditionally it has been the counter-cultural values of the school which have appealed to generations of comic readers, and of course they find it glorious to identify with the naughtiness of Dennis the Menace and despise the goody-goody Cuthbert from Bash Street School. On the other hand, to allow comics to perpetuate and condone offensive racial and gender stereotypes is unacceptable and should be challenged. Stereotyping is not merely a socially convenient, shorthand method of describing groups of people; value judgements are an integral part of the process of categorisation. The readers of comics need to know how and why these stereotypes are constructed and to be aware that in reality they can be hurtful, even when they are vehicles for humour.

With junior aged children it is possible to begin alerting their awareness of just *who* is represented by means of simple content analyses, the results of which can be shown graphically. The children are often surprised that there are more male than female characters and that positive representations of ethnic minorities are invisible. They have never read their comics like this before. Nevertheless, before the power relations which are implicit in the circulation of stereotypical images can be 'read', the processes of how such meanings are produced must be understood. A fairly easy approach to this is to have the children describe their own favourite character at a denotative level. Soon the feature clusters which produce the stereotypical images can be identified and the children become aware of how such images carry connotations which are instantly and unquestioningly read. Pupils can also begin to understand how meaning operates at different levels.

The next step is to place the children on the inside of the processes of production by letting them create a comic strip for themselves. At first they can replicate the conventions and use stereotypical characters to tell a story of their own or one they have heard elsewhere. Once this has been achieved, ask the class to devise comic stories which do not use stereotypes. Destroying the stereotype effectively destroys the genre of the comic, so when one 10 year old in my class tried to create a comic strip featuring a reformed Dennis she found that the only way she could be successful was by replacing him with another stereotypically lovable villain.

Who is represented: a content analysis approach

To initiate discussion relating to the transmission of stereotypical representations on television ask the children to draw up a list of categories showing the kinds of people they meet in their everyday life: old, young; able-bodied, disabled; good looking, plain; rich, poor; happy, sad; white British, other ethnic origin; men, women; and so on. Select a few of these pairs of categories and design a tallying sheet. Taking each pair of categories separately, have the children watch a representative sample of television clips (channel-hopping every

Female	Male
White British	Other Ethnic Group
Disabled	Able-Bodied

minute or so is fine if you are using live television) and record each time they see or hear a person who is a member of that group. In this way the children can see that television does not mirror social diversity. If this activity is repeated with just advertisements, the conventional patterns of media representation are accentuated to the extent that some categories are totally excluded. It is worth mentioning that many commercials for household products have a significantly authoritative, male 'voice over' even when the item is being demonstrated by a woman. This voice can be included in the content analysis.

The values which are inherent in data produced by such content analyses usually form a basis for reflective dialogue. The children in my classes are usually surprised by the statistics which emerge. Ordinary black people rarely feature in advertisements and the poor, the disabled and the old are generally invisible. Even in the afternoon, when programming is often targeted at women, there are usually substantially more men represented.

The following dialogue is an extract from one group of 11 year olds' discussion about the lack of representation of old and disabled people.

Andrew: 'But they do have their own programmes.'
Susan: 'We shouldn't have programmes with *just* old people in them, we should have everyone all together.'
Tony: 'Yes, disabled people are on some programmes, but they're on telly *because* they're disabled.'

Tony's point was that such groups are highlighted *as* groups; that is to say, lifted out of society but not represented as part of the whole social scene.

For those teachers wishing to approach the issue of representation of ethnicity in the media, a teaching pack entitled *My Community* has been designed by the Arts Council for use in primary schools.[19] It begins by focussing on the Irish who have settled in Britain. We rarely consider this group of people to be ethnically separate; they do not pose any 'problem'. Perhaps this is because they are not visibly different from white English people. Multicultural education can sometimes be met with resistant attitudes and so this approach is a gentle and non-threatening introduction.

Prejudiced greetings

Birthday and other such greetings cards also transmit their own brand of ideology. Cards for boys usually portray trains, sport, cars and boats, whereas girls are offered dolls, flowers and cuddly toys. Moreover, very young children's cards are frequently colour coded – blue for boys and pink for girls. Adults' cards follow the same stereotypical themes, and finding an appropriate card for a black child or friend is almost impossible.

The representations of places and times in this medium are also somewhat bizarre. Christmas cards try to engender a sense of security in their historically optimistic images of cosy Victorian scenes, and colonialist British culture is so embedded that cards from Australia have been known to depict towns covered in snow!

How: gender role models

After considering *who* is shown in the media it is necessary to concentrate on *how* certain categories are portrayed and examine some of the underlying power relations which determine media representations. It is expedient to root the activities within the framework of the child's own experiences of media products and maybe it is a good plan to begin by looking at still images.

The following exercise can be adapted to analyse any category and it is possible to use a wide range of media products – newspapers, magazines, advertisements, and so on. I was able to acquire a large selection of *Film Review* magazines which contained photographs of films which were popular with primary pupils. From these magazines I asked the children to work in pairs and choose a picture of a man and a woman from a film which they had seen and enjoyed. Next they described the physical attributes of the people. Consciously searching for details within the images highlights features which are usually assimilated automatically. Working from their descriptions the children can be encouraged to tease out connotative meanings in order to show how implicit values gather together to help construct the existing cultural and ideological power relations.

For example, two 11-year-old girls chose to describe a picture of Sean Connery as James Bond with Kim Basinger from the film *Never Say Never Again*. The girls began by making two columns for their descriptions, which specifically examined the oppositional characteristics.

James Bond
Handsome, he's about fifty five years old, he's strong, he has grey and black hair, he's smiling. He's got a tattoo on his right arm, he's hairy. Wearing a blue shirt and tie, he's mustly (*sic*), wrinkled. He's being clung onto, his mouth is closed, his eyes are squinting, he's gentle with young ladys [*sic*].

James Bond's Girl Friend
Beautiful, wheres (*sic*) make up and ear rings. She has long black hair, she's about twenty three. She's smiling, looking at

the camera, wearing a red swimming costume. She's just right in her size. She's got no wrinkles, she's clinging. Her mouth is open, she's trying to look attractive.

(Eve Johnston and Emma Dean, age 11)

These oppositional characteristics revealed the manner in which the gender roles were being delineated and when asked if the woman could have been 55 years old with grey hair and wrinkles the idea was met with laughter. These images of Bond and 'his woman' were more than photographs of film stars; their attributes could be read as signs and as such they were subject to classification.

Using the same sorts of images it is possible to introduce older juniors to the 'Commutation Test'. This involves taking any one attribute and mentally replacing it with something different. For instance, if the picture were of Rambo holding a vicious-looking dagger, ask the children how it would alter the meaning of the photograph if the knife were to be replaced by a book or a flower. This helps the children to determine which aspects of the picture are significant. It must be pointed out that each element in an image depends for its meaning on its relationship with the other signs.

Often significant imagery – like that of Rambo's knife – operates at the level of a metonym, so even though the viewer may not be able to see any other detail of the scene, the image of the knife will symbolise fear and tension. If photographs which feature well-known and popular stars are chosen, the children are often surprisingly sensitive and enjoy this new way of seeing.

Computers and video games: arenas for the masculine sub-culture

In many primary schools it has been found that the use of computers is dominated by boys[20] and the girls' frustration causes them to reject computer technology. Could the root cause of this be the content of the software? Commercially produced video and computer games are undoubtedly sexist, racist, militaristic and highly competitive.[21] Obviously computer bullies must be controlled in the classroom, but as teachers we need to examine the programs, not necessarily to reject them but rather to raise the children's awareness both of their aggressive nature and of their hidden curriculum of role models which may militate against equal opportunities and reinforce socially damaging attitudes.

One way to initiate a dialogue on how computer games often rely on violent themes is to ask the children to work in pairs or small groups and design a new computer game which is a test of skill but where there are no violent actions or where aggression of every kind results in penalties. This is quite a difficult task because violence in this medium is often equated with an exciting action or a 'win'. Once the children have created their games, these can be compared with a few commercially produced programs. Games often provide a gateway into the computer world, a world which cannot afford to lose potential talent. If pupils find that programs are too aggressive it may be worth their writing to the manufacturers pointing out the need for more acceptable games.

'She-Ra' for little girls and 'He-Man' for boys

Research has suggested that television characters reinforce children's existing sex role stereotypes,[22] so it is worth listening to children's opinions about their current media heroes. Programmes such as *She-Ra* and *He-Man* can be discussed in order to compare how male and female roles are constructed. These are highly rated programmes with primary children and obviously we must respect the children's right to enjoy them. However, it is not destructive to show the children that alternative representations could exist and, after comparing the role of He-Man with that of She-Ra, it is fun to rewrite some of the narratives to equalise the roles. To initiate a discussion, a collection of the gender-stereotyped toys which are central to these types of programmes can be brought into school so that the children can discuss their responses to these greatly sought after, and grossly expensive, artefacts.

Research (funded by Mattel, the creators of He-Man) indicated that boys from the ages of 3 to 7 spend a quarter of their time fantasising about battles between good and evil. It was also found that about 30 per cent of the programme's audience was girls – hence the birth of She-Ra together with her unicorn (with the combable mane).

Just as Supergirl was an appendage of the Superman legend, She-Ra is the twin sister of warrior Prince Adam, alias He-Man, who is an embodiment of honour, strength, commanding leadership and wisdom. With bulging muscles he defends the weak with the assistance of a token black male companion and his attractive female helper who sensually blinks her long eyelashes at He-Man's handsome features and golden hair. She-Ra, although beautiful and brave, appears to draw her power from a masculine, authoritative, god-like presence whose disembodied voice speaks to her when she is in extreme difficulty. Is this supposed to be her twin or is it some other divine presence? Both the language and the technical conventions which construct the representations are different. For example, the clear blue flash of the word 'He-Man' is in contrast to the pretty sparkles around the word 'She-Ra'. These words appear at intervals in the narrative, denoting that they are about to perform some superhuman feat.

Both programmes purport to have a high ethical code and at the end of each film we have a character emphasising the moral of the story. These are sometimes amazingly at odds with the inherently stereotypical messages of the programmes. For instance, we are exhorted not to make the same mistake as the cat woman, who failed to be trusting because the people in the story were different. Instead, she concludes that just because someone is of a different race or religion it does not mean that they are untrustworthy and she says we must not judge people by their appearance.

These homilies raise some questions. Although advertising is dealt with in the previous chapter, it is necessary to pause a moment to remember that He-Man, She-Ra and other such animations – *GI Joe, Thundercats, Transformers, Teenage Mutant Hero Turtles* – are centred around the concept toy or what is known in the industry as the 'licensed character'. That is to say, the toy and its image can be licensed out to appear on anything from wallpaper to school lunch boxes. Today, I asked my class to give me a list of artefacts which featured the comic cat Garfield – there was not room on the blackboard to record them all. Tom Engelhardt's *The Shortcake Strategy*[23] explains the intriguing history of this industry.

However, to return to the issue of the homily, could it be a justification for the continuing existence of these programmes?

From 1969 to 1983 in America, advertising in this form was not allowed, but in 1981 President Reagan appointed Mark Fowler (a member of his presidential election campaign team) as head of the FCC (Federal Communications Commission). Fowler believed that it was time to think about broadcasters, not as public trustees, but in terms of big business. He said 'television is just another appliance. It's a toaster with pictures'. So it was no surprise that, under the cloak of deregulation, the FCC allowed even children's programmes to be surrounded by as many commercials as the television company chose; there was to be no time limit per hour. This was carte blanche for Mattel, Hasbro and other toy manufacturers to broadcast their half-hour animations starring their 'licensed characters', together with their highly buyable accessories.

Talk to the children in any primary school today and the effectiveness of this advertising is pellucid. A class or school survey, where the data can be represented graphically, will reveal the current favourites. Mattel sold 35 million He-Man figures in 1984 alone – that works out at 66.4 each minute! The children usually possess collections of these toys, for the narratives stress socially desirable skills of team work and cooperation. She-Ra needs her unicorn and He-Man must have a Skeletor, and new characters can be always created if the sales figures drop.

At the moment these kinds of programmes are legitimate, but will questions be raised about their validity in the future, by those wishing to safeguard the quality and variety of children's viewing? Will they be allowed to flourish on the strength of their 'high moral tone' which is exemplified by the homily?

In order to facilitate the identification of the significant visual images as well as the linguistic and musical conventions which construct the gender roles of characters such as He-Man and She-Ra, the pupils can be asked to watch extracts from these animations bearing the questions in Worksheet 10 in mind. (Obviously in the future the questions will need to be adapted to match the children's new favourite animations.)

Examining the portrayal of violence in these kinds of animations also bears fruit. Usually it is of a highly ritualistic nature and as a result is unconvincing. Violence is simply equated with the power to dominate. Nevertheless, what do the cataclysmic explosions signify? Are they intended to represent nuclear

Worksheet 10

1 *How does He-Man's battle cat differ from She-Ra's unicorn? Describe them both.*

2 *What difference would it make if the colours of the twins' clothes were exchanged? Look at how colour signifies good and evil, strength and weakness in the stories.*

3 *Who is more capable of rescuing those in danger – She-Ra or He-Men? Why?*

4 *Listen to the music and some of the sound effects on the two programmes. Are they similar or do they differ?*

5 *Are He-Man and She-Ra equally violent? Make a list of the acts of violence in each programme.*

6 *Turn the sound off for a couple of minutes during each programme. This might help you to spot more differences in the way the characters are created.*

7 *Do the girls and the boys in the class agree about the programmes? Would anyone like to change anything about the programmes?*

devastation? With older children it may be worth comparing these representations with the comic strip book by Raymond Briggs, *When the Wind Blows*.[24]

Watching programmes such as these and talking about them with boys and girls is an enlightening experience. When we see why the children enjoy these cartoons and empathise with the characters we are in a better position to understand the media's influence in reinforcing young people's perceptions of gender roles and other social realities.

Representations of enchantment

The racism, sexism and so on expressed in animated cartoons such as *He-Man* and *She-Ra* are a little subtler than that transmitted by the time-honoured medium of folk and fairy stories. Nevertheless there are similarities. The excellent publication *Changing Stories*[25] explores how cultural values in these traditional stories can be identified. The booklet provides teachers with carefully selected short stories and worksheets designed to examine our expectations of princes, princesses, old women, and so on; also stories are included which break the rules of the traditional folk lore. Over the centuries socially desirable and punishable behaviours have been inscribed within the medium of fairy stories and these may well have helped to modify children's behaviour and show them what to expect in society. Other elements of the genre have nourished the child's fantasy world and emotional and psychological development,[26] perhaps in a similar way to the current television animations.

Children still enjoy hearing fairy stories read aloud and it is fun to compare the traditional concept of a princess with the real life ones as depicted on television and in newspapers and magazines.[27] Images of delicate, submissive, beautiful princesses from books can be compared with real princesses who commit traffic offences, fall from horses in cross-country races or pilot helicopters, and these in turn can be compared with modern fairy stories like those of Babette Cole.[28] Finally we might pose the more fundamental, if somewhat subversive question – why should we have princesses at all and does awarding them our attention reinforce their right to retain their ascribed status?

Does reality imitate fiction?

It has been claimed that media fictions establish images of some sections of society, for example the police force. Just how are law and order portrayed? Crime fiction and thrillers have been popular for ages and it has been estimated that a quarter of all paperbacks sold in Britain and America are in this genre.[29] Since the 1950s there has been a succession of police dramas on television. However, the avuncular image of George Dixon – the friendly, honest local 'bobby' with his happy home life – has been superseded by the more realistic *Z Cars*, *The Sweeney*, *Starsky and Hutch*, *The Professionals* and currently *The Bill*. These series increasingly represent the central characters (with whom we are presumably expected to empathise), as operating above the law and police violence is presented as the norm. Is this fair? Is it gritty realism or merely a way of attracting large audiences? The force itself finds the images of uncouth, loud-mouthed, drunken policemen, who are often shown to be cutting legal corners, as both damaging and unreal and has found it necessary to disclaim the realism in expensive newspaper advertisements in order to inform the public and potential new recruits.

But can a few advertisements counter the build-up of dramatic images and do these portrayals of our heroes determine the way the police handle their power?

Primary children do enjoy these crime series but it is edifying to ask their opinions of the realism the programmes attempt to convey. This is an extract from a conversation I taped recently with a group of fourth-year juniors.

Susan: 'Bergerac, he's tough, he's always on a case.'
James: 'The funny thing is that you don't see policemen having a *really* exciting case all the time.'
Jane: 'He nearly always gets a case on his day off.'
James: 'You can almost predict what's going to happen next.'
Andrew: 'In *The Equaliser* right, there was a man and he took a shot, he missed and he was really close, but when The Equaliser shot, he got it.'

Soap opera: bubbles or actuality?

Realism is of central importance in the genre of soap opera. Part of the illusion is usually achieved through the creation of closely knit communities where the social values are often reminiscent of a possibly mythical pre-war working-class Britain.[30] The audience is positioned as eavesdroppers who learn the intimate emotional circumstances of the characters' personal social relationships. The viewers are able to empathise and soon are enmeshed in the plot as 'insiders'. The realism is created within each member of the audience and we are convinced that our lives and the lives of the characters in Albert Square, Coronation Street or Brookside Crescent progress symbiotically. As Dorothy Hobson points out,[31] the time in the serial is restricted to calendar time but not to the time of day – we certainly do not expect the characters to cease their existence when we are not watching them. It is just that the wave lengths do not allow us the privilege of tuning in.

Soap operas are increasingly popular with primary children and it is an ideal genre to analyse if we wish to explore how television's dramatic techniques function to create realism. It is worth explaining to the children that soap operas began as radio programmes in the 1930s in America and that they were sponsored by the makers of detergents. The intention was to gain an audience of women to whom they could sell their soap powder. Consequently women were represented in positive roles, the world was generally that of the home and the family, and the progress of interpersonal relationships was awarded a high profile. Even though soap opera has evolved to match the real world, to a great extent it has still retained many of its original characteristics.

A survey of favourite soaps can be made and the results represented graphically. Older children can undertake research amongst their peers to find out why they enjoy soaps. Some of the most usual answers to these questions are that the children want to know what will happen next, that we like to pry into other people's homes and lives and that the acting is 'very good'. A while ago a child in my class wrote this:

> The people who watch soap operas say that they don't be-
> lieve in them but maybe they believe in them more than they
> really think. Even though they know that there is no such
> place as Albert Square there is a little candle burning slowly
> inside them, making them believe that maybe there is.
> Because this candle is made of fire, it spreads so much that it
> is known that people stop the actor who plays Arthur in
> EastEnders in the streets and say things like 'There is no
> reason to be unemployed you know, there are plenty more
> jobs on offer if you look hard enough'.
>
> (Abaigeal Offord, age 10)

That 'little candle' was apparently burning inside the whole class because *EastEnders* was their favourite programme and their reason for liking it was because it was like 'real life'. My current class feel the same about *Neighbours* and *Home and Away*.

Another effective way to open up the discourse is for every-one in the class (including the teacher) to watch the same episode of a popular soap and the following day in school predict what will happen next on the evidence of what is feas-ible both from a dramatic perspective and from our joint knowl-edge of how the various characters usually react. If a drama lesson can be arranged, the children may work in groups to discuss their predictions and act them out. These dramatisations can then be shared with the whole group.

Whilst the resolving episode is being watched also ask the

children to count how many scene changes occur. Like most television programmes, the soap opera appears to be a seamless whole, but it is really a patchwork of highlighted reality. Soaps 'may not be like life, but they're like television'.[32] When the children in my class returned to school the following day, we all agreed that the episode we had chosen to watch had around twenty-five scene changes, although these traced the progression of only about four interrelated storylines.

At this stage it is a good idea to ask the pupils to write an impossible episode for a soap opera of their choice. In other words, have them break the rules. The characters could behave inappropriately or in ways which are outside the scope of that particular soap. This activity helps to establish the conventions which exist to maintain the stability of the illusion of reality. We can extend this understanding by asking the children to watch their favourite soap and make a list of the ways in which it departs from real life. The following is a selection of written comments produced by the group of fourth-year juniors with whom I worked:

> 'Far too many drastic and unbelievable things happen in a small space of time in such a small community.'
>
> 'In *EastEnders* there are hardly any real children – in my street there are about twenty children.'
>
> 'On soap operas they don't show everything. For example they don't show characters going to the toilet. They just show the bits that we like to be nosey about.'
>
> 'In the election period people *never* say who they would vote for, probably because there are clearly some good people and some clearly bad people [characters in the soap opera]. If the clearly bad people voted conservative, because it's very true to life, some [real] people might change their minds about voting conservative.'

The title sequences of soap operas operate to create a sense of place and they help to seduce us into a familiar, soothing and non-threatening environment where we can vicariously, and perhaps cathartically, experience domestic crises or enjoy the intrigue of a love affair, all from the safe comfort of our own arm chairs. Analysing title sequences highlights the sophistication of these harbingers of escapism into a world we often know better than our own.

Before watching a selection of title sequences the questions in Worksheet 11 may help the children focus their critical awareness. It is a good idea to tape-record the discussion as the ideas may be lost if we wait for the children to write them down. The quotations that follow were thoughts spawned by my group of 10 and 11 year olds.

> 'On *Coronation Street* the music was played by a trumpet, usually quite a loud, exciting instrument but because it is very slow and morbid, it brings across a very grey mood.'
>
> '*EastEnders* showed the river Thames from a bird's eye view, it didn't have many technical events, the camera sort of twirled round and round until we could see the whole of the river.'
>
> '*Dynasty* was a lot longer than the others and was different because the screen is split up. In one column is the character and behind that is the environment.'
>
> '*Emmerdale Farm* was very well done with beautiful sunsets and animals and white doves. I wouldn't watch it because it seems a bit too civilised and sunnydayafternoonish and looks like it's come straight out of another butter advert.'

Worksheet 11

1 *What does the title sequence tell us about the programme's content?*
2 *How do the cuts and fades help create the atmosphere?*
3 *In what ways is a title sequence like an advertisement? (For example, there are often a similar number of technical events, that is to say: cuts, pans, zooms and so on.)*
4 *Listen to the music without watching the screen. What do you learn?*
5 *Watch the title sequences with the sound turned down. What does this tell you?*
6 *Are there any differences between British soap opera title sequences and those from America and Australia?*
7 *Are there any words on the screen which help you to predict what kind of programme will follow?*
8 *Look at a title sequence of a soap with which you are not familiar. Does it make you want to watch the programme?*

The popular press, women's journals and children's magazines devote a considerable amount of space to both the on- and the off- screen relationships, problems and leisure activities of soap opera stars and, as Charlotte Brunsdon suggests, much of this material helps to sustain and reinforce the fiction's reality.[33] Many articles in the tabloid newspapers encourage the confusion between the actors and their fictional roles and this is further aided by the occasional guest appearances by real people; for example, Princess Margaret and Terry Wogan have both taken part in *The Archers*. At key moments in the soap opera's history – the five hundredth show, or maybe the marriage or the death of a character – photographs of past episodes are produced. Owing to the long life of programmes, the familiar characters are able to have aged and developed as a result of their experiences. So looking through these photographs is like browsing through our own family album and we are encouraged to reminisce. We remember what we ourselves were doing when, in the early days of *Coronation Street*, Martha Longhurst, Minnie Cauldwell and Ena Sharples were drinking stout in the Rover's Return. Our history and that of the soaps become interwoven.

Over a period of about a week, ask the children to collect as many written articles about soap opera stars as they can. The collection is usually vast and the sources range from the local and national press and 'free' newspapers to the children's own magazines such as *Look In*. The class can be divided into small groups to read and categorise these articles. They can then examine the ways in which the characters are able to step out of the soap but to some extent remain in role, and how this blurring of realities strengthens our belief in their fictional existence.

Once these preliminary activities have been accomplished, it is great fun for the boys and girls to create their own soap opera. The approach which I intend to describe is just one way and obviously it depends on the age and ability of the pupils. It must be said that it can be time consuming but if you do try I hope you will receive the same kinds of rewards as I experienced.

The first task is to establish the scenario of a tightly knit community which the children can reproduce. For example, my class decided to set their action in a village school. Each child was given a named character to play and they had to write a description of their own role. These descriptions were then shared with the whole class so that everyone knew how to respond to the characters. The children need to listen attentively and it is necessary to negotiate some of the characterisations to avoid repetition. Great care must be taken by the pupils not to create stereotypical cardboard characters and all of the decisions should be reached democratically.

The second task is to select about four or five themes, the intention being that each group of about six students will create one thread of the narrative which will eventually be woven into the episode. Again, themes must address plausible topics. We looked at the press to see if we could glean any clues and decided to consider the issue of a threat of school closure because of falling rolls and financial cut-backs; the second thread was a sponsored jog to raise money for equipment for the classrooms; the third theme was to be the fact that Dutch Elm disease was causing trees to fall; and, lastly, there was the preparation for sports day. Each group can be asked to write its script in about four sections.

The script writing is noisy! It has to be because the children must coordinate their action and inter-group communications need to be maintained. After each section of the script is written, it should be read aloud to enable each group to make any necessary alterations to maintain the flow of the story. At least a week is needed to complete the writing of the scripts and a further week is required for rehearsing the acting. Art work and music should be produced for the title sequence and the actual video-recording demands at least two days.

Even though the resulting film looks nothing like a professional soap opera, it is still enjoyed by the children and their parents. In any case it is not the product which matters but rather the fact that the children have explored the process of how realism is constructed by the media. Throughout the activities there is no question of disparaging the genre; rather we all appreciated its particular form of realism a little more and this enhanced our pleasure. The children enjoy seeing how the dramatic devices construct the illusion. Under normal circumstances these devices almost always escape our notice, but when we have experienced the process of construction we can begin to understand how they work.

Stories and senses

Each medium requires a unique set of technical devices to create realism, and radio is no exception. It is relatively easy for the children to produce a short radio drama as the only equipment needed is an audio tape recorder which has a hand-held microphone. Although radio is not generally popular with primary children, most do possess radios and sometimes BBC Radio for Schools broadcasts dramas and stories. By comparing how the medium differs from television and film it becomes clear how producers may find radio financially and creatively liberating. For instance, fantasy worlds can be created in sound alone. As one girl said:

> You don't need to learn words for a radio play – you couldn't have a script in front of you in a [television] soap opera. Because your audience only hears you, there's no need for scenery, costumes or props. You can have great fun with sound effects. I really enjoyed making the play. The finished result was excellent, it sounded really realistic.
>
> (Alex-jo Dawson, age 9)

This child was beginning to learn how to separate the techniques of the medium from the content and to consider how they affect the structure of the product.

To create a radio play it is advisable for the children to work in groups of five or six. The following points need to be highlighted. First the listener cannot see the action, so it is important for characters to describe their surroundings and each other whilst making these descriptions unobtrusive and a natural part of the play. Secondly, it is sensible to keep the storyline simple enough to follow and, thirdly, the actors' voices should be differentiable. If a second tape recorder is available, pre-recorded sound effects (dogs barking, babies howling, telephones and so on) can be produced at home.

To investigate further how the medium determines the shape of the narrative, it is useful to select a story from a book which is also available on video and compare the differences between the two media. The children can then cast themselves in the role of television directors, select a short scene from a favourite book and produce storyboards, like that on p. 132, to show how this could be created in the medium of film.

CONCLUSION

Laura Krasny Brown[34] says that, from an early age, children recognise that books are written by an author and that not everything in a book is to be believed. She suggests that this may be because the children write their own stories. However,

Marie Bath
Age 8   Story board for Woof!

Action : Reaching for his t-shirt

Dialogue : "I bet I'm ready before
            Roy"

Camera Angle : medium shot

Music : soft

1

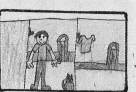

Action : Roy looking down at
         Eric

Dialogue : "Now Eric you've changed
            into a dog"

Camera Angle : two shot

Music : soft

2

Action : Roy coming out of his
         locker

Dialogue : "Woof Woof"

Camera Angle : two shot

Music : none

3

Action : Swimming attendant chasing
         Eric

Dialogue : "Get this dog out of
            here now

Camera Angle : side

Music : none

4

Action : Eric eating a ice lolly

Dialogue : They are not saying
           anything

Camera Angle : two shot

Music : none

5

in the medium of film and television, smooth editing and tech-
nologically advanced special effects mean that the production
processes are invisible. If it is our intention to unpack the
techniques so that young people can consider how the world is
presented as reality by the media, it is vital that we enable
children to experience the construction of narrative in as many
media as possible.

Chapter 6

Media institutions

Media Education in English – 'Producers and audiences –
Who produced this text, and why? For whom is it made, and
how will it reach them? What will they think of it?'[1]

We have to recognise that the media are sites for struggle
between conflicting interests, and ownership/management
power is not absolute, monolithic or uncontested.[2]

AUDIENCES AND ECONOMICS

It has been suggested that whenever we teach about a text we
also teach about the institution which produced it.[3] To some
extent this is true but the teaching is latent, and possibly
counter-productive. Whenever I have asked groups of primary
pupils who, for instance, funds the television programmes we

have been analysing in school, I have received replies that reflect the children's seeming lack of knowledge and lack of interest in this aspect of the medium.

Teacher: 'Have you any idea why the BBC isn't supposed to advertise?'

Susan (11): 'They haven't got enough money.'

Teacher: 'Where do the BBC get their money from?'

Tony (11): 'From people watching telly, paying rent, tax.'

Teacher: 'Have you paid any tax to the BBC?'

Children together: 'No.'

Susan (11): 'We've paid the tax man.'

Teacher: 'Where does the money come from to make the programmes we've seen today?'

Children: 'Banks, bank loans, electricity bills, the mayor, the director, the channel, the queen.'

Alan (11): 'The licence fee.'

Teacher: 'To whom do we pay the television licence?'

Sarah (9): 'It goes to the government and they spend money on making programmes, getting the costumes ready.'

Robert (9): 'The government send it out to each television programme – each channel.'

Many of the children's homes now have channel and satellite television and the future promises more changes, so the organisational compositions and patterns of control of broadcasting are likely to become increasingly complex. Although no media education programme could claim to be complete without addressing the issue of media institutions, in general primary children cannot be expected to unravel every political knot and economic tangle which bind the media industries together. Nevertheless, it is possible to raise pupils' awareness of the underlying influences of the institutions.

This is a very short chapter and merely describes a series of activities which I have found to be successful with the junior age range. However, this is an approach which I believe lays solid foundations so that, at a later stage of education, the children's learning can be extended in ways which enable them to understand more about the fundamental principles which govern the selection of media output and how this relates to the overall structures and the power and control of media institutions.

A PRACTICAL APPROACH

The television audience

It is sensible to centre the practical work around television as this is the medium with which the children are most familiar. It is then advantageous to focus specifically on the notion of audience. Approaching media institutions from this perspective allows the children to analyse certain 'key moments'.[4] For example, the selection procedures of the programme planners as they construct the television schedules (and, incidentally, the audiences) can be simulated so as to question the 'taken-for-grantedness' of television scheduling, which is determined by complex market forces and intricate legal regulations.

Mapping the companies

Before embarking on the simulation exercise it is a good idea to allow the children to learn a little about contemporary structures of television broadcasting. In the future teachers will need to adapt the activity suggested in this chapter to accommodate the changes which deregulation and technological advances will no doubt bring, but it has been predicted that the actual patterns of programme viewing are unlikely to change significantly in the next decade, although the viewing will probably be spread over a larger number of differently funded channels.[5]

At the time of writing I have found that initially it is profitable to concentrate on ITV's fifteen companies (not including TV-am) as they are more obvious to viewers than the BBC's four Network Production Centres and the nine Regional Television Stations. This background information does not lend itself to discovery learning, so, after showing the logos of the companies to the children, it is necessary to explain that each company caters for an area of the country whose regional interests it claims to reflect. It must also be explained that programmes made by any one company are shown in other regions and usually simultaneously. The children will have seen the logos on their television screens and, if a large outline map of Britain is produced and the logos are given to the class, a game can be played. This involves the pupils in seeing how many of the logos they can recognise and then, by deduction, placing each

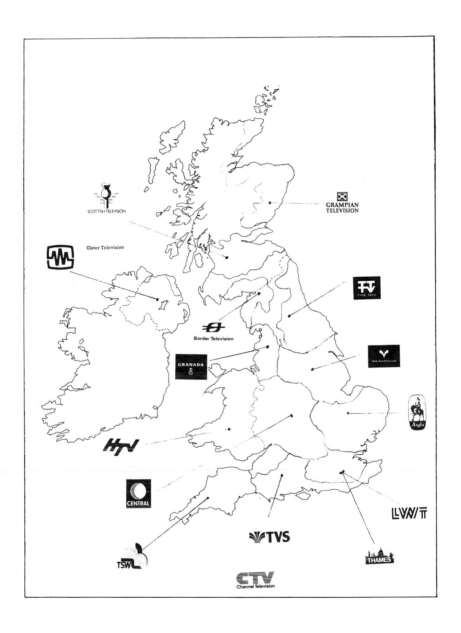

company's logo on the outline map. Promotional booklets produced by the IBA are of assistance here,[6] and of course an atlas will help the children with the task.

Having tried the activity with all ages in the junior school it is astonishing how much knowledge can be drawn from any group of children, even when at first they might have appeared to know very little. The following is an extract from a transcript of an audio-taped group discussion. The children were mixed-ability 7 year olds.

Timothy:	'I've seen lots of those signs.'
Barry:	'Yes, they're the different television companies. That's Central – the main one we see, they broadcast from Nottingham.'
Timothy:	'That's Thames – *Rainbow* is on there'
Barry:	'That's Yorkshire – when I lived in Newark we got Yorkshire Television.' [Because Newark is in the north of Nottinghamshire, Barry placed the Yorkshire logo above the *Central* one.]
Jill:	'That's Tyne Tees TV.'
Teacher:	'What's the Tyne?'
Kate:	'It's a river and it's in Newcastle.'

The older juniors can colour in the areas but I have found that the younger children find it easier just to Blu-tack the logos onto the maps. Another approach to this activity is for the teacher to draw the shapes of the areas the companies serve onto an outline map and then cut these out and let the children put the map together like a jigsaw. In this way geographical inaccuracies are avoided. With the older age ranges it can be mentioned that these companies are often part of diversified industries[7] and that Thames, Central, Yorkshire, Granada and London Weekend are the dominant companies and are known as 'The Big Five'.

Planning the schedules: a simulation for 9–11 year olds

Divide the class into mixed-ability groups each comprising about six children and give them samples of a week's independent schedules for Channel 3. Ask two children to adopt the role of people who go to work in the daytime; two other children need to empathise with adults who are at home all day; and the remaining children in the group should be themselves.

The task is for each group to design a schedule for a Friday evening (1600–2100), bearing in mind that many ITV programmes may be viable only if they can capture a large enough audience which can be sold to the advertisers. Therefore the children should aim to maximise viewing statistics wherever possible. It is sensible to limit the time for this activity to about 1 hour. After each group has completed its schedule, a plenary session should be arranged when all of the schedules may be shared and one final composite schedule negotiated with the teacher cast in the role of the chairperson.

During this meeting the teacher can point out the public service responsibilities of the IBA; for instance, that there should be no more than 2 hours of non-British material,[8] and that the authority insists on an average of 2½ hours of serious/factual programmes in peak viewing time each week.

Many scheduling techniques for retaining an audience are learnt naturally in the process of the simulation. For instance, in the following transcript of the plenary discussion of a group of 9 year olds it is apparent that they saw the benefit of 'bridge programmes' which carry viewers from one programme to the next, the desirability of variety, the family viewing policy, the need for regular news and the fact that films have high ratings.

Linda: 'Let's have *The Roxy* on at a quarter to five because that's for teenagers and then you'll keep them and the children watching up to the News and then some of the people will watch all three programmes.'

Sarah: 'You could get them all watching earlier if you put on *Splash*.'

Andy: 'Look, you've got two cartoons on there together, I think we should split them. Put the *Krypton Factor* on at 6 o'clock and then you'll keep the men [*sic*] who have been watching the News.'

Linda: 'Yes and then you can have *The Two of Us*. That's a comedy, it's very funny and I think that grown-ups would enjoy it just as much as children do.'

John: 'Well I think we should have a film at 7 o'clock.'

Linda: 'Yes, yes *The Silver Streak*.'

   [At this point the children had become very excited.]

John:	'No way, James Bond, *A View to Kill* is much better. That'll fetch a big audience because it's never been on television before.'
Andy:	'I agree with John, James Bond is well known and well liked and you'll get the majority of people watching, more than for films you've re-shown.'
Jane:	'Well I think we shouldn't have a film until after seven thirty. We could show *Auf Wiedersehen Pet* first. It's about these builders and it *is* funny.'
Nadine:	'Oh yes, but you'd have to be careful because it's got some words in it you're not allowed to use.'
Arnold:	'Well, I tell you what, let's put on *Nature Watch*.'
Andy:	'Ugh, teenagers wouldn't watch that, we don't want to lose *them*.'

It is a good idea to tape-record these 'meetings' so that the teacher can use the tapes as a basis to help the children reflect upon their own dialogue and learning.

A competitive schedule

The next stage of the simulation is for the class to return to their original groups, this time armed with the final ITV Friday evening's schedule and samples of the week's BBC 1 schedules. Their task now is to simulate the BBC programme planners' meeting.

However, before the children decide on their programmes it is expedient to furnish them with some information which will facilitate the production of a highly competitive schedule. As the previous extract from the children's discussion demonstrated, they may discover many of the techniques incidentally, but process-orientated learning must also strive to be efficient. The adoption of a progressive pedagogy is not an excuse for allowing pupils to waste time re-inventing the wheel. Time can be saved if the children are taught about:

(1) 'Channel loyalty' – the tendency of viewers to watch one channel for several programmes once they have turned on the set.
(2) 'The inheritance factor' – the fact that a high proportion of an audience will watch a little of the programme which follows a popular show.
(3) 'Pre-echo' – because viewers do not wish to miss the start of

a favourite programme, they may tune in early and see the last few minutes of the preceding show.

(4) 'Pre-scheduling' – this ploy involves beginning an attractive show a few minutes before a competitive programme on another channel and so capturing the viewers.[9]

(5) Regular patterns of programming can attract a regular following.

(6) A combination of 'pre-echo' and 'inheritance' can form a 'hammocking' effect – that is to say, a weak programme is broadcast between two popular shows.

(7) It is sometimes difficult for the children to understand why the BBC needs to compete for audiences when it receives the statutory licence fee, but once it is realised that the corporation has to justify, to the government of the day, any request for an increase in this fee, the reason for the fierce competition is plain. At this point it is worth explaining how The Broadcasters Audience Research Board (BARB) calculates the ratings.[10]

The task of designing a BBC schedule which will compete successfully with the previously chosen ITV programmes can now be realised and if anything the group and class meetings are even more exciting (and noisier) than when the children planned the ITV schedules.

REFLECTION

Although the activities suggested in this chapter are merely an introduction to one small way in which media institutions function in our society and how our television diet is regulated, they do enable the children to be aware of the complexity of the process and that someone produces the programmes for specific audiences and why. Also the pupils begin to learn something about themselves as media consumers and in the process realise how competition often provides not choice but, rather, more of the same types of programmes.[11]

Conclusion

> We might ask, as a criterion for any subject taught in primary school, whether when fully developed, it is worth an adult's knowing, and whether having known it as a child makes a person a better adult.[1]

When Bruner's questions are directed to media education, I believe the answers to both are resoundingly positive. The children see the purpose of their learning and their enthusiasm for the activities is invariably infectious. When parents and governors are told what media education hopes to achieve, there is generally a high level of support; however, it is advisable to write explanatory notes to parents if we wish pupils to carry out media research at home. This kind of homework often opens up new and critical dialogues between parents and children which can only be applauded.

As the preceding chapters have shown, most media education is investigative learning which allows children to develop their understanding of how they are addressed by the mass media and how social and ideological meanings are created and circulated. How the pupils interpret and respond to the learning is entirely individual, and all viewpoints should be considered with respect.

For teachers who are introducing media education into their classrooms for the first time, I would like to conclude this book by hoping that they and their pupils gain as much pleasure from it as I and my classes have received.

Appendix
Primary media education and the National Curriculum

For each chapter which addresses a practical approach to media education, I have added a section that highlights how the suggested classroom activities are, at the time of writing, related to the National Curriculum. These sections are intended to be neither exhaustive nor uniform in their presentation; rather they are signposts to guide planning and record keeping.

Key to abbreviations used:

AT = Attainment target
E   = English
KS1 = Key Stage 1
KS2 = Key Stage 2
L   = Level
M   = Mathematics
NAT = proposed New Attainment Target (mathematics and science)
NSG = Non-Statutory Guidance
POS = Programmes of Study
S   = Science
T   = Technology

2 TEACHING VISUAL LITERACY

English

9.2 Media education . . . enlarges pupils' critical understanding of how messages are generated, conveyed and interpreted in different media.

9.8 We have considered media education largely as part of the exploration of contemporary culture alongside more traditional literary texts.

9.9 Media education . . . deals with fundamental aspects of language, interpretation and meaning. It is therefore consonant with the aims of English teaching.

See helpful suggestions and notes in the NSG:

C12 8.11 (June 1989) Children can be encouraged to think of watching television or films, or looking at pictures, as a kind of reading. By looking closely at visual images and discussing exactly what they can see . . . children can begin to see how most still and moving images are organised on purpose, and how visual conventions and symbols are used.

D9 (June 1990) Names and Terms KS1 & 2 . . . explore and classify badges, coats of arms, logos . . .

D16–17 Media Education in English (the whole of section 4.0 is relevant):

4.1 Media education contributes to most aspects of the English curriculum. Practical and analytical work on media will involve negotiation, problem-solving, group decision-making, selection and editing, all of which enhance children's abilities in reading, writing, speaking and listening. . . .

4.8 . . . The questions English teachers ask about written texts can also be asked about photographs or radio programmes. In studying and producing media texts, pupils will also consider how they produce meaning: how sounds and images can be combined to form a narrative or the characteristics of particular genres. . . .

4.13 As in other aspects of English, pupils should be helped to reflect on their work, and be encouraged to make explicit the reasons for the choices they have made, considering their effects on real or potential audiences.

(See suggested work on Taking Photographs, KS1 D19.)

Attainment targets

AT1 Speaking and Listening
L 2d; 4b.

AT2 Reading
16.23 Activities should ensure that pupils appreciate the signifi-

cance of print and the fact that pictures and other visual media can also convey meaning, e.g. road signs, logos . . . (*The Cox Report – English for ages 5–16*) 2d; 3e; 4c; 5c.

AT3 Writing
L 2c; 3d; 4c.

Mathematics

AT12 Handling Data [NAT 5]
Pupils should collect, record and process data.
L 4 i) [NAT L 4 ii) 8 iii)] specify an issue for which data are needed; collect, group and order discrete data using tallying methods with suitable equal class intervals and create a frequency table for grouped data.

AT13 Handling Data [NAT 5]
Pupils should represent and interpret data.
L 2 i) [NAT L 2 iii)] construct, read and interpret block graphs and frequency tables
L 3 i) [NAT L 3 iii)] construct and interpret bar charts
ii) create and interpret graphs (pictograms) where the symbol represents a group of units
L 4 ii) [NAT L 4 iv)] construct, read and interpret a bar-line graph for a discrete variable
L 5 i) [NAT L 5 iv)] construct and interpret a pie chart from a collection of data with a few variables. . . .

Science

Working with light-sensitive paper is useful in achieving the very important AT1 Exploration of science [NAT 1] e.g. L 2 i) ask questions and suggest ideas of the 'how', 'why' and 'what will happen if' variety
L 3 ix) describe activities carried out by sequencing the major features
L 4 ii) formulate testable hypotheses
vi) Carry out an investigation with due regard to safety
x) describe investigations in the form of ordered prose, using a limited technical vocabulary
L 5 ii) identify and manipulate relevant independent and dependent variables, choosing appropriately between ranges, numbers and values

Activities with optical illusions and toys can answer the following requirements:

AT15 [NATs 4 and 5] Using light and electromagnetic radiation
L 4 i) know that we see objects because light is scattered off them and into our eyes
L 6 ii) be able to give an account of the structure of the eye.

Technology

The work on animation can help fulfil these requirements.

AT1 Identifying Needs and Opportunities
L 2 a) describe what they have observed or visualised and found in their exploration

AT2 Generating a Design
L 3 c) draw from information about materials, people, markets and processes and from other times and cultures to help in developing their ideas

AT3 Planning and Making
L 2 a) describe to others how they are going about their work

AT4 Evaluating
L 1 b) describe to others what they have done and how they have done it
L 2 a) discuss with teachers and others how satisfied they are with their design and technological activities, taking into account their original intention and how they went about their task
L 4 c) comment upon existing artefacts, systems or environments, and those from other times and cultures, including appearance and use of resources

NSG (April 1990)
C11 Media education can be used to teach part of the design and technology programme of study . . . [Children] should understand how advances in technology have contributed to the making of media products and how the choice of medium influences the impact of the product on the audience. Pupils will learn from the forms and conventions of media and how products can be designed to make them attractive to the audience.

History

Historical Sources KS1 Core History Study Unit 1

5.3 Visual material
Teachers should help pupils to increase their understanding of the past by the study of a wide range of pictures, photographs, maps and other visual material.

5.4 Oral history
Teachers should give pupils opportunities to explore the history of the recent past through listening to parents, grandparents and other adults talking about their experiences . . . (*National Curriculum History Working Party* – Final Report, 1990).

AT1 Knowledge and understanding of history
L 2 identify differences between past and present times

AT2 Interpretations of history
L 2 show an awareness that different stories about the past can give different versions of what happened. (Detect differences in two adults' accounts of the same past event)
L 3 distinguish between a fact and a point of view
L 5 recognise that interpretations of the past, including popular accounts, may differ from what is known to have happened

AT3 The use of historical sources
L 1 communicate information acquired from an historical source. (Talk about what they see in an old photograph)
L 2 recognise that historical sources can stimulate and help answer questions about the past
L 3 make deductions from historical sources. (Make simple deductions about social groups in Victorian Britain by looking at the clothes people wore)
L 4 put together information drawn from different historical sources

POS KS1 Unit 1
Links with AT2
* develop awareness of different ways of representing past events, for example: pictures, written accounts, films, television programmes . . .
* distinguish between different versions of events, for example: different accounts by pupils of events which happened in school a week, month or year ago

POS KS2
Links with AT2
* investigate differences between versions of past events, for example: how pictures and wall charts give different impressions of life in Ancient Egypt

Art

Children in the world today learn as much through visual images as they do through words. The understanding and use of visually communicated information, gathered from a whole range of sources, has become a basic skill. Pupils need to learn that pictures and symbols can have several meanings, and that different interpretations of them are possible and valid in a modern industrial society and in a multicultural world.

Developing the art curriculum

Visual literacy
3.8 Young people need to be visually literate to operate successfully in society. Visual images enter everyone's life through the mass media, they carry information and ideas within popular culture. . . . Images and objects can embody the ideas, the values and the technology of their communities. In order to sustain its culture, each generation must learn to understand its received images and interpret them in the light of its own experience.

AT1 Understanding and Evaluating Art
POS KS2
A. Describing and evaluating own work
Pupils should be taught to: iii) understand how their research and their use of skills contribute to their making and their ability to make personal statements
C. Art and design in a wider context
Pupils should be taught to: ii) explain why the work of artists and designers is influenced by where and how they live and work

AT2 Making
POS KS2
B. Formal elements

Pupils should be taught to: ii) explore and experiment with composition. Use a viewfinder or a camera to organise or select a composition

AT3 Observation, Research and Developing Ideas
KS1
Pupils should be able to: c) describe and discuss their response to a range of visual sources
KS2
c) use written and spoken language to help them undertake and develop visual enquiry and to describe their perceptions

POS
B. Collecting and using information from secondary sources
KS1
Pupils should be given the opportunity to: i) build up personal and class collections of images, objects and artefacts. Collect photographs of self and family . . .

Cross-attainment target projects

KS1 'It's Me'
1 studying family photographs to identify family likenesses and differences
3 comparing photographs of themselves as babies with their appearance now

KS2 'Our Community'
3 working in groups to make a photomontage of focal points in the community . . .
7 collecting information about, and recording, the different typefaces used by local shops and businesses; making charts to explain their differences and effectiveness.

3 LEARNING ABOUT NEWS

The English National Curriculum provides ample support for teaching about news, but the activities suggested in this chapter also help to fulfil many other requirements of the document. The following extracts are just a few which legitimise learning about news. Although I have set an upper limit of levels 5/6, as all primary teachers know, children's progression in language is not linear and we should not restrict our pupils to achieving at these levels.

English

AT1 Speaking and Listening
L 3d; 4c; 5b,c,d

POS KS1
3 Planned situations and activities should cover:
* working with other children and adults involving discussion with others; listening to, and giving weight to, the opinions of others; perceiving the relevance of contributions; timing contributions; adjusting and adapting views expressed
4 All activities should:
* by informal and indirect means, develop pupils' ability to adjust the language they use and its delivery to suit particular audiences, purposes and contexts . . .
5 The range of activities should . . . include:
* securing responses to visual and aural stimuli, e.g. pictures, television, radio, computer, telephone, making use of audio and video recordings as appropriate

KS2
Pupils should learn how to:
* express and justify feelings, opinions and viewpoints with increasing sophistication
* assess and interpret arguments and opinions with increasing precision and discrimination
* present factual information in a clear and logically structured manner in a widening range of situations and discriminate between relevance and irrelevance, and recognise bias.

NSG
B3 (1990) At KS2 group activities which require extended discussion, speculation and the development of reasoned argument include the writing of books for younger children, the compiling of newspapers, the devising of role play or scripted drama. . . .

AT2 Reading
L 2f; 4c; 5c,e

POS KS1
7 . . . the pupils should be guided so as to:
* appreciate the significance of print and the fact that pictures and other visual media can also convey meaning

NSG KS2
B4 There will be a progressive widening of the range of reading available to include more challenging material such as poetry not specifically written for children, as well as magazines and newspapers.

AT3 Writing
L 2b; 5a,e

POS KS1
10 Pupils should write individually and in groups, sharing their writing with others and discussing what they have written, and should produce finished pieces of work for wider audiences.
14 Pupils working towards Level 3 should be taught to recognise that their writing involves:
* decision making – when the context is established
* drafting – when initial thoughts are developed, evaluated and reshaped by expansion, addition or amendment to the text.

KS2
Pupils should continue to have varied and frequent opportunities to write. They should know for whom they are writing.

NSG KS2
B7 Drama can provide a way of extending the range of audiences, by writing within a role play or simulation. It is important that teachers encourage children to talk about their writing, before the final product is completed so that they can learn to handle conventions and match their writing to a particular audience.

D16–17 Media Education in English
4.4 By encouraging pupils to reflect on their own experience as readers and writers of media, teachers will enable them to make their understanding explicit and systematic, and will motivate them to find out more about how the media work.
4.8 Approach 3: producers and audiences
Who produced this text, and why?
For whom is it made, and how it will reach them?
What will they think of it?
4.10 Children should produce media texts – for example photographs, newspapers, audio and video tapes. Practical media work gives pupils a means of expression.

Approaches to the class novel
The suggestions which are offered in *The Cox Report – English for ages 5–16* (June 1989) provide excellent starting points for teaching about the news.
13 Incidents from the story written as news; front pages with a composite of stories relating to central event. Emphasis on reporting from outside the event; what should be selected as 'news'.
Learning features: Translating events into familiar forms. Popularising the text, reporting and journalistic conventions. Creating a distance between characters' perceptions of events and the readers'.
14 Investigative journalism . . . Presenting, selecting, arranging material. Authorial intention and bias. Airing values, making judgements.

Technology

POS KS2
Satisfying needs and addressing opportunities:
* making judgements about products designed and made by others
Developing and communicating ideas:
* develop styles of visual communication which take account of what is to be conveyed, the audience and the medium to be used

NSG
Information Technology (April 1990)

KS2 Communicating information
Pupils . . . can use the word processor to create class newspapers or stories for younger children . . .

Design and technology
2.11 Pupils should experience a range of methods of recording and communicating:
* written (stories, letters, diaries, logs, questionnaires, notes, newspaper articles, storyboards)
* spoken (performance, role play, recorded conversations, interviews, debates, simulated radio programmes)

Art

Cross-attainment target projects

KS2
'Carrie's War'
Work in art and design could include:
1 using local newspaper archives to identify and record changes
in the appearance of the local community resulting from the
Second World War; making drawings, photocopies and photographs to make comparisons between 1945 and 1990.

4 SOME APPROACHES TO TEACHING ABOUT ADVERTISING

English

Aims of the English curriculum

2.16 An objective is to develop children's understanding of the
different ways meanings are conveyed. A traditional concern of
the English teacher has always been to develop the ways in
which children interpret texts, spoken or written, literary or
non-literary, and to increase children's understanding of how
texts convey multiple layers of meaning and meanings expressed from different points of view.
2.17 Children should be able to make sense of how messages
are conveyed in a variety of forms and contexts: in the heritage
of literature written in English, but also in the mass media, in
film and television.
2.25 A 'cultural analysis' view emphasises the role of English in
helping children towards a critical understanding of the world
and the cultural environment in which they live. Children
should know about the processes by which meanings are conveyed, and about the ways in which print and other media carry
values.
2.27 . . . aspects of media education are . . . important for
children in the primary phase, because they can be influenced
by the conventions and assumptions of mass media, and should
learn to recognise this.

Attainment targets

AT1 Speaking and Listening
15.7 Through such media as TV, radio and the cinema, for instance, [children] will see and hear an abundance of information which they will need to evaluate and use judiciously for their own purposes.

POS
15.23 Media work has a particular significance, leading naturally to discussion of how spoken language and visual accompaniment are interpreted; this leads to an understanding of the processes of selection, omission and editing which take place when any programme is prepared. For example in advertising can pupils distinguish the aesthetic from the transactional?

AT2 Reading
16.11 As independence is strengthened, pupils should be encouraged to read more difficult texts and to look not only at what is said, but how meaning is expressed and how effects are achieved in writing.

POS
16.23 ii) Pupils . . . should be shown how to distinguish between fact and opinion in a variety of texts, including newspapers, magazines and advertisements.
N.B. L 5 iii) Pupils should be able to recognise, in discussion, whether subject matter in non-literary and media texts is presented as fact or as opinion.

AT3 Writing
17.20 . . . 'People receive information and misinformation in varying proportions from, amongst others, family and friends, workmates, advertisers, journalists, priests, politicians and pressure groups. A democratic society needs people who have the linguistic abilities which will enable them to discuss, evaluate and make sense of what they are told, as well as to take effective action on the basis of their understanding' (extract from *The Kingman Report* 1988).
For a resumé of the rationale for teaching about the media in general, see Chapter 9 of *The Cox Report – English for ages 5–16*, (1989) which is devoted to Media Education and Information Technology.

Mathematics

Mathematics in the curriculum

A rationale for cross-curricular work – F1

1.1 In life, experiences do not come in separate packages with subject labels. As we explore the world around us and live our day-to-day lives, mathematical experiences present themselves alongside others.

1.7 The incentives for schools to plan cross-curricular approaches in mathematics are clear:
* they reflect the real world in which we live;
* they enable more efficient use of time to be planned for;
* the contribution of mathematics to other areas of the curriculum can be maximised;
* working in a variety of contexts helps pupils to learn.

Attainment targets and the levels of attainment which are supported by activities suggested in this chapter of the book:

AT	Level	NAT	Level
1	3,5	1	3,5
2	4	2	4
3	5	4	4
9	2,3,4,5	5	2,3,4,5
10	4		
12	4,5		
13	2,3,4,5		
14	3,4,5		

Science

POS
Children should use a variety of domestic and environmental contexts as starting points for learning about science.

Attainment targets and levels of attainment which are supported by activities suggested in this chapter:

AT1 L 3 [NAT 1 and 3]
* Pupils should be able to distinguish between a 'fair' test and an 'unfair' test.

AT3 L 4 [NAT POS KS2]
* Pupils should know about the factors which contribute to good

health and body maintenance, including the defence system of the body, balanced diet, oral hygiene and avoidance of harmful substances such as tobacco, alcohol and other drugs.

AT8 [NAT 4] Pupils should develop their knowledge and understanding of models to explain the structure and properties of materials. (Cf. the sections of the chapter devoted to packagings of products and uses of colours.)

Art

Aims
4.1 Art education should: enable pupils to become visually literate: to use and understand art as a form of visual and tactile communication, to have confidence and competence in 'reading' and evaluating visual images and artefacts

ATI Understanding and evaluating art
POS KS2
C. Art and design in a wider context
Pupils should be taught to: i) recognise that there are different kinds of art and design forms because they have been made for different purposes – Compare the different functions of familiar forms such as portraits, postage stamps, posters, television commercials, etc.

5 REPRESENTATIONS OF REALITY

Webs help in the planning of topic work for 'Representations of Reality'. Although I have targeted the centres of interest on soap opera and toy animations at Levels 4 & 5 and the work on comics at Levels 2 & 3, this should not be perceived as a restriction. Naturally the webs can be extended to embrace any other areas the teacher wants to cover with her class. The webs are merely intended to be used as starting points.

Soap opera: 'It'll all come out in the wash'

Levels 4 & 5

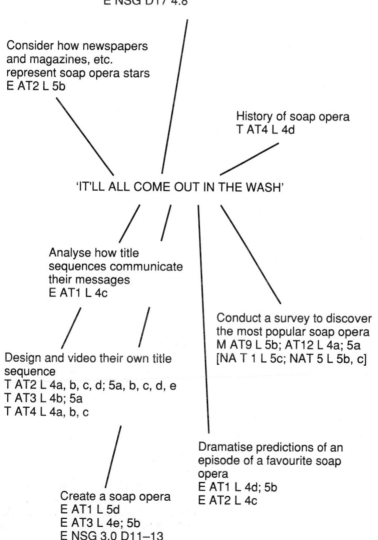

Realism and representation
E NSG D17 4.8

Consider how newspapers
and magazines, etc.
represent soap opera stars
E AT2 L 5b

History of soap opera
T AT4 L 4d

'IT'LL ALL COME OUT IN THE WASH'

Analyse how title
sequences communicate
their messages
E AT1 L 4c

Conduct a survey to discover
the most popular soap opera
M AT9 L 5b; AT12 L 4a; 5a
[NA T 1 L 5c; NAT 5 L 5b, c]

Design and video their own title
sequence
T AT2 L 4a, b, c, d; 5a, b, c, d, e
T AT3 L 4b; 5a
T AT4 L 4a, b, c

Dramatise predictions of an
episode of a favourite soap
opera
E AT1 L 4d; 5b
E AT2 L 4c

Create a soap opera
E AT1 L 5d
E AT3 L 4e; 5b
E NSG 3.0 D11–13

Toy animations: 'We have the power'

Levels 4 & 5

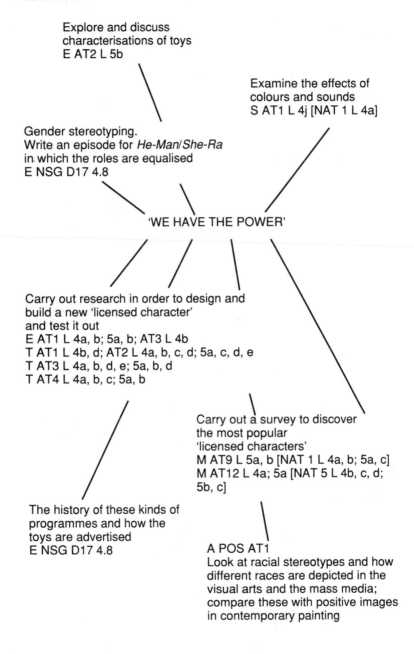

Explore and discuss
characterisations of toys
E AT2 L 5b

Examine the effects of
colours and sounds
S AT1 L 4j [NAT 1 L 4a]

Gender stereotyping.
Write an episode for *He-Man/She-Ra*
in which the roles are equalised
E NSG D17 4.8

'WE HAVE THE POWER'

Carry out research in order to design and
build a new 'licensed character'
and test it out
E AT1 L 4a, b; 5a, b; AT3 L 4b
T AT1 L 4b, d; AT2 L 4a, b, c, d; 5a, c, d, e
T AT3 L 4a, b, d, e; 5a, b, d
T AT4 L 4a, b, c; 5a, b

Carry out a survey to discover
the most popular
'licensed characters'
M AT9 L 5a, b [NAT 1 L 4a, b; 5a, c]
M AT12 L 4a; 5a [NAT 5 L 4b, c, d;
5b, c]

The history of these kinds of
programmes and how the
toys are advertised
E NSG D17 4.8

A POS AT1
Look at racial stereotypes and how
different races are depicted in the
visual arts and the mass media;
compare these with positive images
in contemporary painting

Comics: 'Dennis for ever'

Levels 2 & 3

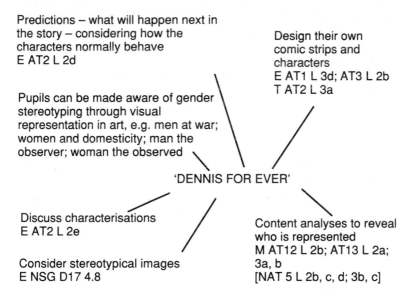

Predictions – what will happen next in
the story – considering how the
characters normally behave
E AT2 L 2d

Design their own
comic strips and
characters
E AT1 L 3d; AT3 L 2b
T AT2 L 3a

Pupils can be made aware of gender
stereotyping through visual
representation in art, e.g. men at war;
women and domesticity; man the
observer; woman the observed

'DENNIS FOR EVER'

Discuss characterisations
E AT2 L 2e

Consider stereotypical images
E NSG D17 4.8

Content analyses to reveal
who is represented
M AT12 L 2b; AT13 L 2a;
3a, b
[NAT 5 L 2b, c, d; 3b, c]

6 MEDIA INSTITUTIONS

Planning television schedules can help to fulfil the following
attainment targets.

English

AT1 Speaking and Listening
L 3c,d; 4b,c,d; 5c,d

AT2 Reading
L 4d; 5d

AT3 Writing
L 3d; 5d

Technology

AT1 Identifying needs and opportunities
Pupils should be able to identify and state clearly needs and
opportunities for design and technological activities through
investigation of the contexts of home, school, recreation, community, business and industry.

AT2 Generating a design
Pupils should be able to generate a design specification, explore ideas to produce a design proposal and develop it into a realistic, appropriate and achievable design.

AT3 Planning and making
Pupils should be able to make artefacts, systems and environments, preparing and working to a plan and identifying, managing and using appropriate resources, including knowledge and processes.

AT4 Evaluating
Pupils should be able to develop, communicate and act upon an evaluation of the processes, products and effects of their design and technological activities and those of others, including those from other times and cultures.

Geography

AT1 Geographical skills
L 2a use geographical vocabulary to talk about places

AT2 Knowledge and understanding of places
L 3b demonstrate that they know the location of their local area within the country in which they live

POS KS1
Geographical skills
3 Pupils should be taught to:
* extract information from, and add to, pictorial maps

Places and themes
6 Pupils should be taught:
* that their own country is part of the United Kingdom, which is made up of England, Wales, Scotland and Northern Ireland

POS KS2
Geographical skills
2 Pupils should be taught to:
* select relevant information from a variety of sources, for example, visitors, photographs, maps, charts, documents, atlases, globes, videos, TV and radio programmes, computer databases, books, newspapers

REFERENCES

Material quoted in this appendix is taken from the following DES documents which are presented in chronological order.

Report of the Committee of Inquiry into the Teaching of English Language – The Kingman Report, 1988.

English for ages 5–16 – The Cox Report, 1989.

Mathematics in the National Curriculum (& Non-Statutory Guidance), 1989.

Science in the National Curriculum, 1989.

English in the National Curriculum (& Non-Statutory Guidance), 1990.

National Curriculum History Working Party – Final Report, 1990.

Technology in the National Curriculum (& Information Technology Capability & Information Technology Capability), 1990.

Art Working Group – Interim Report, 1991.

Geography in the National Curriculum (England), 1991.

History in the National Curriculum (England), 1991.

Mathematics for ages 5 to 16, May 1991.

Science for ages 5 to 16, May 1991.

Notes

Introduction

1 BFI/DES (1989) *Primary Media Education: A Curriculum Statement*, London: BFI.
2 DES (1989) *English for Ages 5–16 – The Cox Report*, London: HMSO.
3 T. Griffin, (ed.) (1987) *Social Trends*, No. 12, Central Statistical Office, London: HMSO.
4 DES (1987) *The National Curriculum 5–16 – A Consultation Document*, Wales: HMSO.
5 R. Curtis, cited in L. Masterman (1985) *Teaching the Media*, London: Comedia Publishing Group.
6 Masterman, ibid.
7 J.D. Wills (1977) Television and political education, unpublished MA thesis, University of York.
8 D. Spender (1980) *Man Made Language*, London: Routledge & Kegan Paul.
9 Schools Council (1983) *Primary Practice*, Schools Council Working Paper No. 75, London: Methuen Educational for the Schools Council.
10 C. Rogers (1983) *Freedom to Learn in the '80s*, Columbus, Ohio: Charles E. Merrill Publishing Co.
11 P. Freire (1970) *Pedagogy of the Oppressed*, Harmondsworth: Penguin Books.
12 DES (1987) op. cit.
13 ibid.

1 Starting points

1 R. Eke (1976/7) Doing film in the primary school, *Screen Education*, No. 21, Winter, pp. 32–4.
2 Ministry of Education (1938) *The Spens Report on Secondary Education*, London: HMSO.
3 Ministry of Education (1959) *The Crowther Report*, London: HMSO.

4 F.R. Leavis and D. Thompson (1933) *Culture and Environment*, London: Chatto & Windus.
5 ibid.
6 R. Hoggart (1957) *The Uses of Literacy*, Harmondsworth: Penguin in association with Chatto & Windus.
7 S. Hall and P. Whannel (1964) *The Popular Arts*, London: Hutchinson.
8 Ministry of Education (1963) *Half Our Future – The Newsom Report*, London: HMSO.
9 DES (1975) *A Language for Life – The Bullock Report*, London: HMSO.
10 L. Masterman (1980) *Teaching about Television*, London: Macmillan.
  J., Hartley, H. Goulden, and T. O'Sullivan (1985) *Making Sense of the Media*, London: Comedia Publishing Group.
  M. Alvarado, R. Gutch, and T. Wollen (1987) *Learning the Media*, London: Macmillan Education.
11 DES (1983) *Popular TV and Schoolchildren*, London: HMSO.
12 R. Barthes (1972) *Mythologies*, London: Cape.
13 DES (1989) *English for Ages 5–16 – The Cox Report*, London: HMSO.
14 A. Bandura, D. Ross, S.A. Ross, (1963) Imitations of film mediated aggressive models, *Journal of Abnormal and Social Psychology*, LXVI, pp. 3–11.
  J.L. Singer, and D.G. Singer (1980) *Television, Imagination and Aggression: a study of pre-schoolers*, Hillsdale, New Jersey: Lawrence Erlbaum.
  L.D. Eron (1980) Prescription for reduction of aggression, *American Psychologist*, 35(3), 1980, pp. 244–52.
  M.M. Lefkowitz, L.D. Eron, L.O. Walder, and L.R. Huesmann (1977) *Growing up to Be Violent*, New York: Permagon Press.
  Surgeon General's Scientific Advisory Committee on Television and Social Behavior (1972) *Television and Growing Up: The Impact of Televised Violence*, Report to the Surgeon General, US Public Health Service, Washington DC: US Government Printing Office.
15 D.G. Singer, D.M. Zuckerman, J.L. Singer (1980) Helping elementary school children learn about TV, *Journal of Communication*, Summer, 30(3), pp. 84–93.
  A. Dorr, S. Browne Graves, and E. Phelps (1980) Television literacy for young children, *Journal of Communication*, Summer, 30(3), pp. 71–83.
  W. Rapaczynski, D.G. Singer, and J.L. Singer (1982) Teaching television: a curriculum for young children, *Journal of Communication*, Spring, 32(2), pp. 46–55.
  L.J. Baron (1985) Television literacy curriculum in action: a long term study, *Journal of Educational Television*, 11(1), pp. 49–55.
  M.E. Ploghoft, and J.A. Anderson (1982) *Teaching Critical Viewing Skills: An Integrated Approach*, Springfield, Illinois: C.C. Thomas.
16 G. Sellar, L. Hoare, B. McMahon, D. Smith (eds) (1987) *Primary Teachers' Resource Book*, Western Australia: Education Department of Western Australia.
17 B. Hodge, and D. Tripp (1986) *Children and Television: A Semiotic Approach*, Cambridge: Polity Press.

18 G. Noble (1975) *Children in Front of the Small Screen*, London: Constable.
19 P. Palmer (1986) *The Lively Audience: A Study of Children Around the TV Set*, Sydney: Allen & Unwin.
20 P. Willis (1971) 'What is new?' A case study in *Working Papers in Cultural Studies*, No. 1, Spring, University of Birmingham.
21 S. Hall (1973) Encoding and decoding in the television message, in S. Hall, D. Hobson, A. Lowe, and P. Willis (eds) *Culture, Media, Language – Working Papers in Cultural Studies 1972–9*, London: Hutchinson in association with the Centre for Contemporary Cultural Studies, University of Birmingham, 1980.
22 R. Barthes (1977) *Image – Music – Text*, London: Fontana.
23 Ploghoft and Anderson op. cit.
24 Hall op. cit.
25 H.M. Enzenberger (1976) *Raids and Reconstructions: Essays in Politics, Crime and Culture*, London: Pluto.
26 Barthes (1977) op. cit.
27 J.S. Bruner (1966) *Towards a Theory of Instruction*, Cambridge, Mass.: Harvard University Press.
28 J.T. Lawton, R.A. Saunders, and P. Muhs (1980) Theories of Piaget, Bruner and Ausubel: explications and implications, *Journal of Genetic Psychology*, 136, pp. 121–36.
29 DES (1989) *Science in the National Curriculum*, London: HMSO.
30 M. McLuhan (1964) *Understanding Media*, London: Routledge & Kegan Paul.
31 A. Toffler (1970) *Future Shock*, London: Bodley Head.
32 K. Jones (1987) *Six Simulations – An Oral Skills Resource*, Oxford: Blackwell.

2 Teaching visual literacy

1 S. Sontag (1973) *On Photography*, New York: Farrar, Strauss & Giroux.
2 J. Berger, S. Blomberg, C. Fox, M. Dibb and R. Hollis (1972) *Ways of Seeing*, Harmondsworth: Penguin Books with the BBC.
3 B. Hodge, and D. Tripp (1986) *Children and Television: A Semiotic Approach*, Cambridge: Polity Press.
4 G. Noble (1975) *Children in Front of the Small Screen*, London: Constable.
5 Hodge and Tripp op. cit.
6 J. Mezirow (1977) Perspective transformations, *Studies in Adult Education*, October, 9(2), pp. 153–64.
7 A. Bethell (1974/5) An approach to the study of images, *Screen Education*, No. 13, Winter, pp. 31–5.
8 E.W. Eisner (1982) *Cognition and the Curriculum: A Basis for Deciding What to Teach*, New York: Longman.
    D. Buckingham (1988) Television literacy: a critique, Paper presented to the 1988 International Television Studies Conference at the University of London Institute of Education.
    M.E. Levison (1986) Reading media, *Educational Forum*, 50(2), Winter, pp. 149–57.

9 M.L.J. Abercrombie (1960) *The Anatomy of Judgement,* Harmonds-worth: Pelican.
10 R.L. Gregory (1966) *Eye and Brain,* London: Weidenfeld & Nicolson.
11 B. Ernst (1986) *Adventures with Impossible Figures,* Norfolk: Tarquin Publications.
12 J. Bruner (1958) Social psychology and perception, in E.E. Maccoby, T.M. Newcomb, E.L. Hartley (eds) (1958) *Readings in Social Psychology,* New York: Holt.
13 E.H. Gombrich (1964) *The Story of Art,* London: Phaidon.
14 From an idea by Barry Ecuyer. Pack available from: 50 Eastwood Drive, Littleover, Derby.
15 See ideas by J.P. Golay (1971) Introduction to the language of image and sound, *Screen Education,* Winter; and R. Eke (1976/7) Doing film in the primary school, *Screen Education,* No. 21, Winter, pp. 32–4.
16 S. Isherwood (n.d.) *The Family Album,* Channel 4: 60 Charlotte Street; London W1P 2AX.
17 B. McMahon, and R. Quin (1986) *Real Images: Film and Television,* Melbourne: Macmillan and Company of Australia.
18 L. Masterman (1980) *Teaching About Television,* London: Macmillan.
19 A. Bethell (1981) *Eyeopeners* (One and Two), Cambridge: Cambridge University Press.
20 Masterman op. cit.
21 R. Barthes (1972) Preface to *Mythologies,* London: Cape.
22 R. Silverstone (1981) *The Message of Television: Myth and Narrative in Contemporary Culture,* London: Heinemann.
23 J. Lewis (1990) Are you receiving me? In A. Goodwin and G. Whannel (eds) (1990) *Understanding Television,* London: Routledge.
24 Worksheets may be obtained from: The National Museum of Photography, Film and Television, Prince's View, Bradford, West Yorkshire, BD5 OTR; Tel. (0274) 727488. Other sheets have been produced by: Robin and Nell Dale Toys, Bank House Farm, Holme Mills, Holme via Carnforth, Lancashire. Excellent recent material – *Making Images Move* – is available price £1 from the Museum of the Moving Image in London.
25 B. Ecuyer (1990) *Animation in the Primary School,* and Jackdaw Media (1990) *Animation,* London: Arts Council.
26 C. Bailly (1985) *Illford Manual of Classroom Photography,* PO Box 21, Southall, Middlesex, UB2 4AB.
27 Berger et al., op. cit.

3 Learning about news

1 D.L. Altheide (1986) *Creating Reality: How TV News Distorts Events,* Beverly Hills: Sage Publications.
2 IBA (1987) *Attitudes to Broadcasting in 1986,* London: Independent Broadcasting Authority.
3 L.M. Jaglom and H. Gardner (1981) The preschool television viewer as anthropologist, in H. Kelly and H. Gardner (eds) *Viewing Children Through Television – New Directions for Child Development,* No. 13, September, San Francisco: Jossey Bass.

BBC (1987) *The BBC's Programme Responsibilities towards Adolescents and Young Adults*, London: British Broadcasting Corporation.

4 D.R. Anderson, L.F. Alwitt, E.P. Lorch and S.R. Levin (1979) Watching children watch television, in G.A. Hale and M. Lewis (eds) (1979) *Attention and Cognitive Development*, New York: Plenum.

5 S. Hood (1980) Introduction, in L. Masterman, *Teaching about Television*, London: Macmillan.

6 L. Masterman (1980) *Teaching about Television*, London: Macmillan.

7 R. Barthes (1977) *Image–Music–Text*, London: Fontana.

8 Y. Davies (1986) *Picture Stories*, London: British Film Institute.

9 M. Simons, C. Bazalgette and A. Bethell (n.d.) *Teachers' Protest*, distributed by the Society for Education in Film and Television for the ILEA English Centre: SEFT, 29 Old Compton Street, London, W1V 5P1.

10 D. Walker (1985) Writing and reflection, in D. Bond, R. Keogh and D. Walker (eds) (1985) *Reflection: Turning Experience into Learning*, Sydney: Kogan Page.

11 S. Cohen and J. Young (eds) (1973) *The Manufacture of News*, London: Constable.

12 L. Hughes (1990) Real or fake? No longer in the eye of the beholder, *Guardian*, 4 September 1990, p. 7 EG.

13 K. Jones (1984) *Graded Simulations*, vol. 1, London: Blackwell.

14 Altheide op. cit.

    J. Galtung and M. Ruge (1973) Structuring and selecting news, in Cohen and Young op. cit.

    Glasgow University Media Group (1980) *More Bad News*, vol. 2 of *Bad News*, London: Routledge & Kegan Paul.

    S. Hall, C. Critcher, T. Jefferson, J. Clarke and B. Roberts (1978) *Policing the Crisis: Mugging, the State and Law and Order*, London: Macmillan.

    P. Schlesinger (1978) *Putting 'Reality' Together – BBC News*, London: Constable.

15 ibid.

16 Masterman op. cit.

17 G. Dyer (1978) Teaching about television interviews, *Screen Education*, No. 27, Summer, pp. 38–51.

18 Galtung and Ruge op. cit.

19 L. Masterman and P. Kiddey (1983) *Understanding Breakfast TV – TV Study Unit No. 1*, Nottingham: M.K. Media Press.

20 T. Davidson and J. Ashton (n.d.) *Video in the Classroom: Some Outline Strategies*, Clwyd Media Studies Unit in conjunction with Wrexham Community Video Project.

4 Some approaches to teaching about advertising

1 A. Huxley (1928) *Advertising and Selling*, 7 April 1928, p. 49.

2 U. Eco (1979) Can television teach? *Screen Education*, No. 31, Summer, pp. 15–21.

3 Annan Committee (1977) *Report of the Committee on the Future of Broadcasting*, London: HMSO.

4 DES (1989) *English for ages 5–16 – The Cox Report*, London: HMSO.
5 B. Dwyer, and B. Walshe (1984) *Learning to Read the Media*, Rozell, NSW Australia: Primary English Teaching Association.
6 C. James (1985) Marketing and advertising to school-age children, What do we know about the children's market? *Admap*, May, No. 240, pp. 254–9.
7 R.P. Adler, G.S. Lesser, L.K. Meringoff, T.S. Robertson, J.R. Rossiter and S. Ward (1980) *The Effects of Television Advertising on Children*, Massachusetts: Lexington Books.
8 J. Cunningham (1989) Sweet icing on the cake, *The Guardian*, 16/10/89.
9 R. Williams (1974) *Television: Technology and Cultural Form*, London: Fontana/Collins.
10 P. Conrad (1982) *Television: The Medium and its Manners*, Boston: Routledge & Kegan Paul.
11 S. Ward, B. Daniel, B. Wartella, and E. Wartella (1977) *How Children Learn to Buy*, Beverly Hills: Sage Publications.
12 D. Smythe (1981) *Dependency Road: Communications, Capitalism, Consciousness and Canada*, New Jersey: Ablex Publishing Corporation.
13 J. Hartley (1982) *Understanding News*, London: Methuen.
14 J. Williamson (1978) *Decoding Advertisements: Ideology and Meaning in Advertising*, London: Marion Boyars Publishers Ltd.
15 J. Mander (1978) *Four Arguments for the Elimination of Television*, New York: Morrow Quill.
16 Ministry of Education (1989) *Media Literacy: Resource Guide*, Ontario: Ministry of Education.
17 B. McMahon, and R. Quin (1984) *Exploring Images*, East Perth, Western Australia: Brookland Pty.
18 J. Berger, S. Blomberg, C. Fox, M. Dibb, and R. Hollis (1972) *Ways of Seeing*, Harmondsworth: Penguin Books with the BBC.
19 T. Vestergaard, and K. Schroder (1985) *The Language of Advertising*, Oxford: Blackwell.
20 Conrad op. cit.
21 P. Taylor (1985) *The Smoke Ring: Tobacco, Money and Multinational Politics*, London: Sphere Books.
22 R. Marchand (1985) *Advertising the American Dream: Making Way for Modernity 1920–1940*, Berkeley: University of California Press.
23 BRAD [*British Rate and Data*] (1984) August.
24 Cited in L. Masterman, and P. Kiddey (1983) *Understanding Breakfast TV – TV Study Unit No. 1*, Nottingham: M.K. Media Press.
25 ibid.
26 L. Masterman (1985) *Teaching the Media*, London: Comedia Publishing Group.
27 ibid.
28 M. McLuhan (1964) *Understanding Media*, London: Routledge & Kegan Paul.
29 M. Stoppard (1989) *TV Times*, 7–13 October 1989.
30 V. Matthews (1987) The not-so-hidden persuaders, *Guardian*, 25 May 1987.

31 M. Schudson (1984) *Advertising, The Uneasy Persuasion: Its Dubious Impact on American Society*, New York: Basic Books.
32 The Code of the Advertising Standards Authority.
33 Smythe op. cit.

5 Representations of reality

1 M. Alvarado, R. Gutch, T. Wollen (1987) *Learning the Media: An Introduction to Media Teaching*, London: Macmillan.
2 J. Ellis (1982) *Visible Fictions: Cinema, Television, Video*, London: Routledge & Kegan Paul.
3 R. Williams (1983) *Keywords: A Vocabulary of Culture and Society*, London: Flamingo.
4 J. Root (1986) *Open the Box*, London: Comedia Publishing.
5 T. Eagleton (1983) *Literary Theory – An Introduction*, Oxford: Blackwell.
6 G. Gerbner (1970) Cultural indicators: the case of violence in television drama, *Annals of the American Association of Political and Social Science*, 338, pp. 69–81.
7 T. Griffin (ed.) (1988) *Social Trends*, No. 16, Central Statistical Office, London: HMSO.
8 M. Butler, and W. Paisley (1980) *Women and the Mass Media: Sourcebook for Research and Action*, New York: Human Sciences Press.
9 F.E. Barcus (1977) *Children's Television: An Analysis of Programming and Advertising*, New York: Praeger.
    L.J. Busby (1975) Sex-role research on the mass media, *Journal of Communication*, 25, pp. 107–31.
    J.D. Nolan, J.P. Galst, and M.A. White (1977) Sex bias on children's television programs, *Journal of Psychology*, 96, pp. 197–204.
    O.G. O'Kelly (1974) Sexism in children's television, *Journalism Quarterly*, 51, pp. 722–4.
    R.W. Poulos, S.E. Harvey, and R.M. Liebert (1976) Saturday morning television: a profile of the 1974–5 children's session, *Psychological Reports*, 39, pp. 1047–57.
10 R. Dohrmann (1975) A gender profile of children's educational TV, *Journal of Communication*, 25, pp. 56–65.
11 G. Gerbner, L. Gross, M. Morgan, and N. Signorielli (1980) The mainstreaming of America: Violence Profile, No. 11, *Journal of Communication*, 30, pp. 10–29.
12 D.E. Fernie (1981) Ordinary and extraordinary people: children's understanding of television and real life models, in H. Kelly and H. Gardener (eds) *Viewing Children Through Television: New Directions for Child Development*, No. 13, San Francisco: Jossey Bass Inc.
13 K. Durkin (1985) *Television, Sex Roles and Children*, Milton Keynes: Open University Press.
14 B. Hodge, and D. Tripp (1986) *Children and Television: A Semiotic Approach*, Cambridge: Polity Press.
15 C. Craggs (1989) Media Education and the Junior School Curriculum, unpublished MPhil thesis: University of Nottingham.

16 J. Winship (1980) Sexuality for sale, in S. Hall, D. Hobson, A. Lowe and P. Willis (eds) *Culture, Media, Language – Working Papers in Cultural Studies, 1972–9*, London: Hutchinson.

17 R. Welch, A. Huston-Stein, J. Wright, and R. Plehal (1979) Subtle sex role cues in children's commercials, *Journal of Communication*, 29(3), pp. 202–9.

18 B. McMahon, and R. Quin (1984) *Exploring Images*, East Perth, Western Australia: Brookland Pty.

19 N. Rathod (1990) *My Community*, London: Arts Council.

20 C. Mihill (1990) Girls feel terminal boredom thanks to computer bullies, *Guardian*, 25 August 1990.

21 P.M. Greenfield (1984) *Mind and Media – The Effects of Television, Computers and Video Games*, London: Fontana.

22 J.N. Sprafkin, and R.M. Liebert (1978) Sex-typing and children's preferences, in G. Tuchman, A.K. Daniels and J. Benet (eds) *Hearth and Home: Images of Women in the Mass Media*, New York: Oxford University Press.

23 T. Engelhardt (1986) The shortcake strategy, in T. Gitlin (ed.) *Watching Television: A Pantheon Guide to Popular Culture*, New York: Pantheon Books.

24 R. Briggs (1982) *When the Wind Blows*, London: Hamish Hamilton.

25 D. Denaro (1984) *Changing Stories*, London: ILEA English Centre.

26 B. Bettelheim (1975) *The Uses of Enchantment*, London: Thames & Hudson.

27 C. Goodwin (1989) Investigating a character type, in C. Bazalgette, *Primary Media Education: A Curriculum Statement*, London: BFI/DES.

28 B. Cole (1986) *Princess Smartypants*, and (1987) *Prince Cinders*, London: Hamish Hamilton.

29 A. Farrugia (n.d) *TV Representations of the Police*, Clwyd Media Studies Unit; available from: County Civic Centre, Mold, Clwyd CH7 1YA.

30 R. Rosen (1986) Search for yesterday, in Gitlin (1986) op. cit.

31 D. Hobson (1981) *Crossroads: The Drama of a Soap Opera*, London: Methuen.

32 P. Conrad (1982) *Television: The Medium and its Manners*, Boston: Routledge & Kegan Paul.

33 C. Brunsdon (1984) Writing about soap opera, in L. Masterman, *Television Mythologies – Stars, Shows and Signs*, London: Comedia/MK Media Press.

34 L.K. Brown (1986) *Taking Advantage of the Media*, Boston: Routledge & Kegan Paul.

6 Media institutions

1 DES (1990) *English in the National Curriculum, Non Statutory Guidance*, London: HMSO, p. D17, §4.8.

2 L. Masterman (1985) *Teaching the Media*, London: Comedia Publishing.

3 M. Alvarado, R. Gutch, and T. Wollen (1987) *Learning the Media*, London: Macmillan Education.

4 G. Branston (1984) TV as institution: strategies for teaching, *Screen Education*, 25(2), March/April, pp. 85–94.
5 P. Barwise, and A. Ehrenberg (1988) *Television and its Audience*, London: Sage Publications.
6 Independent Broadcasting Authority (1987) *A Pocket Guide to Independent Television and Radio*, London: IBA.
7 C. Bazalgette, J. Cook, J. Hawken, J. Heywood, P. Simpson, and J. Smoker (n.d.) *The Companies You Keep*, London: BFI.
8 At the time of writing the actual figures are as follows: there should be no more than 14.5 per cent of material from countries other than Britain and the EC and a maximum of 5 hours of non-EC programmes in the peak hours of the schedule in any one week.
9 More detailed information can be found about points (1)–(4) in L. Masterman (1980) *Teaching about Television*, London: Macmillan.
10 For a simple explanation see G. Slater (1987) *Planning the Schedules*, London: Hodder & Stoughton.
11 R. Williams (1979) Television and teaching: an interview with Raymond Williams, *Screen Education*, No. 31, Summer, pp. 5–14.

Conclusion

1 J.S. Bruner (1960) *The Process of Education*, Cambridge, Mass.: Harvard University Press.

Bibliography

This bibliography is an attempt to provide a balanced reading list representing the various schools of thought.

Adler, R.P., Lesser, G.S., Meringoff, L.K., Robertson, T.S., Rossiter, J.R. and Ward, S. (1980) *The Effects of Television Advertising on Children*, Massachusetts: Lexington Books.
  Although of the effects school of thought, this contains useful reference material. The chapter on children's ability to distinguish television commercials from programme content (Meringoff and Lesser) is particularly interesting.
Altheide, D.L. (1976) *Creating Reality: How TV News Distorts Events*, Beverly Hills: Sage Publications.
  Altheide argues that the very processes of news production promote a way of regarding events which is distorting.
Alvarado, M., Gutch, R. and Wollen, T. (1987) *Learning the Media*, London: Macmillan Education.
  The chapters on institutions, race, narrative, class and gender provide provoking reading; however, the authors scatter the text with political viewpoints which could be alienating for some teachers.
Apple, M.W. (ed.) (1982) *Cultural and Economic Reproduction in Education – Essays on Class, Ideology and the State*, London: Routledge & Kegan Paul.
  Chapter 7 is a noteworthy essay by Todd Gitlin on hegemony in transition.
Barthes, R. (1972) *Mythologies*, London: Cape.
  A seminal collection of essays, each of which analyses some aspect of popular culture. The final chapter, 'Myth today', although an intellectually demanding read, explains, amongst other things, how language not only predetermines meaning but reflects dominant power relations.
Barthes, R. (1977) *Image-Music-Text*, London: Fontana.
  An influential collection of essays. 'The Rhetoric of the Image' is particularly valuable.

Bazalgette, C., Cook, J., Simpson, P. (n.d.) *Selling Pictures*, London: British Film Institute.
A teaching pack which is a resource for exploring the production and circulation of stereotypical images. The student booklet (aimed at the secondary sector) is entitled *The Companies You Keep* and contains excellent material relating to the issue of media ownership.

Belsey, C. (1980) *Critical Practice*, London: Methuen.
Chapter 6, 'Towards a productive critical practice', is relevant to media teachers.

Berger, J., Blomberg, S., Fox, C., Dibb, M. and Hollis, R. (1972) *Ways of Seeing*, Harmondsworth: Penguin Books with the BBC.
An important and well-illustrated text which makes important links between popular culture and fine art.

Bethell, A. (1974/5) An approach to the study of images, *Screen Education*, No. 13, Winter, pp. 31–5.
A short, inspiring and thoroughly readable article.

Bethell, A. (1981) *Eye Openers* (One and Two), Cambridge: Cambridge University Press.
Two slim booklets containing activities which facilitate visual literacy. Book One is especially suitable for use at Key Stage 2 of the National Curriculum.

British Film Institute/Department of Education and Science, (1989) *Primary Media Education: A Curriculum Statement*, London: BFI.
A fine introductory text for work at Key Stages 1 and 2, it contains accounts of classroom practice written by teachers.

Brown, L.K. (née Meringoff) (1986) *Taking Advantage of the Media – A Manual for Parents and Teachers*, Boston: Routledge & Kegan Paul.
A positive text which discusses how each medium shapes narrative differently.

Brown, R. (ed.) (1976) *Children and Television*, London: Collier Macmillan.
A collection of essays showing how television has become part of the matrix of influence on children's understanding of their world and how they interact with the medium.

Brunsdon, C. and Morley, D. (1987) *Everyday Television: 'Nationwide'*, Television Monograph No. 10, London: British Film Institute.
Although now rather dated, this detailed analysis of the programme offers some especially useful writing about ideology.

Bryant, J. and Anderson, D.R. (eds) (1983) *Children's Understanding of Television: Research on Attention and Comprehension*, London: Academic Press.
The contributors to this collection of essays include well-known American researchers in the field and Chapter 12 is a review of American television literacy programmes.

Buckingham, D. (ed.) (1990) *Watching Media Learning – Making Sense of Media Education*, London: Falmer Press.
This presents accounts of classroom research which look at some of the difficulties and contradictions between the theory and practice of media teaching and it questions the assumptions which teachers sometimes make about the understandings which the children already possess.

Clarke, M. (1987) *Teaching Popular Television*, London: Heinemann Educational Books in association with the British Film Institute.
Although aimed at the secondary sector, the book contains many teaching strategies and ideas which are helpful.

Cohen, S. and Young, J. (eds) (1981) *The Manufacture of News*, revised edn, London: Constable.
A collection of critical essays about news production.

Collett, P. and Lamb, R. (1985) Watching People Watching Television, Oxford: unpublished Report to the IBA.
This research involved placing cameras to watch how people watch television. The findings revealed that the activity was far from passive; rather, people were seen to come and go and often television viewing was a secondary activity.

Conrad, P. (1982) *Television: The Medium and its Manners*, Boston: Routledge & Kegan Paul.
An exploration of television's various realities: talk shows, soap operas, game shows, advertisements, news and drama.

Cowley, J. (1987) *Switch On*, Leamington Spa: Scholastic Publications.
A primary school pack of thirty-two attractive photocopiable worksheets and a student reader. However, the activities are prescriptive, sometimes unrealistic and blatantly inoculative against media effects. For example, one section requires the children to stop watching television for two days.

Cullingford, C. (1984) *Children and Television*, Hampshire: Gower.
A thorough and balanced review of the effects research which looks at children's tastes, viewing habits and styles, attention to television, heroes and heroines, recall and recognition. There are also chapters on education and television and on television as a conveyor of information and propaganda.

Curran, J., Ecclestone, J., Oakley, G. and Richardson, A. (1986) *Bending Reality – The State of the Media*, London: Pluto Press.
A set of polemic essays on subjects such as media representations of racism, the peace movement, pornography and homosexuality. The authors – who include Stuart Hall, James Curran, Philip Whitehead, Peter Golding and Tony Benn – argue that the problems of representation are connected with the ownership and control of the media.

Davies, Y. (1986) *Picture Stories*, London: British Film Institute.
A teaching pack which contains introductory notes, slides and pages of photographs to use for practical activities. It is exactly what it claims; that is to say, starting points for media education. Having used the activities once, teachers can progress to develop their own materials.

Day-Lewis, S. (ed.) (1989) *One Day in the Life of Television*, London: British Film Institute/Grafton Books.
On 1 November 1988, people throughout Britain wrote accounts of their day's television experiences. This selection from the resulting 15 million words includes the opinions of ordinary people and those from within the television industry.

Denaro, D. (1984) *Changing Stories*, London: Inner London Education Authority English Centre.
A source book of folk and fairy tales and worksheets which raise the issue of how girls and boys are expected to behave. The stories can be a sensitive way of looking at how media representations shape perceptions of gender roles.

Department of Education And Science (1983) *Popular Television and School Children*, London: HMSO.
An official report by a group of teachers. The research was concerned with television's representations of adult life and the influences they have on young people. The findings suggested that all teachers should be involved in discussing television with children.

Dorfman, A. and Mattelart, A. (1971) *How to Read Donald Duck – Imperialist Ideology in the Disney Comic*, New York: International General.
A controversial look at imperialism in children's comics.

Dorr, A. (1986) *Television and Children: A Special Medium for a Special Audience*, Beverly Hills: Sage Publications.
An American review of the recent television effects literature.

Durkin, K. (1985) *Television, Sex Roles and Children*, Milton Keynes: Open University Press.
A thorough evaluation of the research into the complex issue of how television may influence children's understanding of gender roles.

Dwyer, B. and Walshe, B. (1984) *Learning to Read the Media*, New South Wales, Australia: Primary English Teaching Association.
This contains accessible chapters on how to read television, radio and newspapers.

Dyer, G. (1982) *Advertising as Communication*, London: Methuen.
An examination of how advertising communicates within its cultural and economic setting. Recommended.

Eagleton, T. (1983) *Literary Theory – An Introduction*, Oxford: Blackwell.
An intellectually demanding but enlightening introduction to literary theory. Such terms as phenomenology, hermeneutics, reception theory, structuralism, semiotics and post-structuralism are explained.

Fiske, J. (1982) *Introduction to Communication Studies*, London: Methuen.
This book goes a long way to explain the models, theories and concepts involved and is well worth reading.

Freire, P. (1970) *Pedagogy of the Oppressed*, Harmondsworth: Penguin Books.
A valuable read for any teacher. Freire argues that the essentially political nature of education means that it can be used either to liberate or to oppress. He suggests that the teacher's task is to facilitate genuine reflective dialogue rather than cramming the learner with information. He proposes that oppressive regimes socialise and structure the thought of the people so that liberation is seen in terms of actually becoming the oppressors.

Gitlin, T. (ed.) (1986) *Watching Television: A Pantheon Guide to Popular Culture*, New York: Pantheon Books.
A collection of essays including 'The Shortcake Strategy' by Tom Engelhardt, which provides a history of how the media market toys.

Glasgow University Media Group (1976) *Bad News*, London: Routledge & Kegan Paul; (1980) *More Bad News*, London: Routledge & Kegan Paul; (1982) *Really Bad News*, London: Writers and Readers; (1985) *War and Peace News*, Milton Keynes: Open University Press.
Four volumes which explore bias in news broadcasting.

Goodwin, A. and Whannel, G. (eds) (1990) *Understanding Television*, London: Routledge.
A collection of essays which discuss such issues as hegemony, ideology, and the history and business of television organisations.

Greenfield, P.M. (1984) *Mind and Media – The Effects of Television, Computers and Video Games*, London: Fontana.
A hopeful book, which suggests that the media contribute positively to children's learning.

Hall, S., Hobson, D., Lowe, A. and Willis, P. (eds) (1980) *Culture, Media, Language, – Working Papers in Cultural Studies 1972–9*, London: Hutchinson in association with the Centre for Contemporary Cultural Studies, University of Birmingham.
Contains a significant chapter on encoding and decoding by Stuart Hall.

Hall, S. and Whannel, P. (1964) *The Popular Arts*, London: Hutchinson.
For those teachers interested in tracing the evolution of media education, this book shows how the attitudes of the time were changing from a negative view of the popular arts towards a discrimination between them.

Harpley, A. (1990) *Bright Ideas – Media Education*, Warwickshire: Scholastic Publications.
This is a book of easy-to-follow, well-illustrated, practical ideas which are particularly useful at Key Stages 1 and 2 of the National Curriculum. It includes work on image analysis, advertisements, watching television, the news, communication and production and there are a number of reproducible worksheets.

Hartley, J. (1982) *Understanding News*, London: Methuen.
An informative text for readers who wish to consider news values. Chapter 2, 'Reading the news',is a good introduction to the study of signs.

Hartley, J., Goulden, H. and O'Sullivan, T. (1985) *Making Sense of the Media*, London: Comedia Publishing.
This is an ambitious series of ten booklets which presume to offer a comprehensive, cross-phase media education curriculum and certainly they contain some extremely valuable information and ideas. However, the publication is marred by poor illustrations and page layouts, and the package is expensive (£25).

Himmelweit, H., Oppenheim, A. N. and Vince, P. (1958) *Television and the Child*, London: Oxford University Press.
A piece of timely research into children's viewing habits and a valuable text for comparing how these habits have changed over the past decades.

Hobson, D. (1981) *Crossroads: The Drama of a Soap Opera*, London: Methuen.
An enlightening book which defines soap opera and describes the audience responses to *Crossroads*, which was a particularly despised programme.

Hodge, B. and Tripp, D. (1986) *Children and Television: A Semiotic Approach*, Cambridge: Polity Press.
A carefully documented study of how children interpret television, and one which recognises the positive role television plays. The book is a welcome challenge to the effects theorists who, the authors believe, have been asking the wrong questions. The research seeks insights into children's understanding rather than positivistic proofs.

Hoggart, R. (1957) *The Uses of Literacy*, Harmondsworth: Penguin in association with Chatto & Windus.
One of the first books to open serious dialogue about the role of popular culture. It is a readable book which draws on Hoggart's own childhood experiences of northern England.

Hood, S. (1980) *On Television*, London: Pluto Press.
A polemical critique of television, the first chapter, 'The screen', is a useful introductory read.

Howe, M. (1977) *Television and Children*, London: New University Education.
Although now dated, Howe's book allows the reader to understand how media influences were regarded in the 1970s.

Kelly, H. and Gardner, H. (eds) *Viewing Children through Television – New Directions for Child Development*, San Francisco: Jossey Bass Inc.
A collection of articles which include 'The preschool television viewer as anthropologist' (L.M. Jaglom and H. Gardner – an analysis of viewing in the early years showing how the child is able to organise the medium and make connections between its content and his/her experience) and 'Schemata for understanding television' (W.A. Collins).

Leavis, F.R. and Thompson, D. (1933) *Culture and Environment*, London: Chatto & Windus.
This text is an account of how not to teach about the media; however, it is important as it opened the debate and had a great influence in the early days of media education.

Lloyd, P. (1987) *Soap Opera*, Brighton: Spartacus Press.
This booklet presents a practical approach to teaching about soap opera. Although more suitable for the secondary years there are some useful ideas for primary work.

Lusted, D. and Drummond, P. (eds) (1988) *TV and Schooling*, London: British Film Institute.
A collection of essays produced after the publication of the DES report *Popular TV and Schoolchildren*. This book is divided into five sections which explain the context, the broadcasters' perspectives, critical perspectives, television, the media and education, and finally there is a section on the DES report itself.

McLuhan, M. (1964) *Understanding Media*, London: Routledge & Kegan Paul.
   Although written in 1964, the seminal first chapter, 'The medium is the message', is essential reading.
McMahon, B. and Quin, R. (1984) *Exploring Images*, East Perth, Western Australia: Brookland Pty.
   A well-illustrated book intended for students but it is also of value to teachers who wish to help children begin learning how to analyse images. Chapter 2 is a helpful guide to semiotics; Chapter 4 is useful for understanding the concept of myth; Chapter 5 addresses itself to cartoons.
McMahon, B. and Quin, R. (1986) *Real Images: Film and Television*, Melbourne: Macmillan and Company of Australia.
   An impressively practical, readable and well-illustrated book with information on codes and conventions, genre and ideology. Although intended for senior pupils who are studying film and television, the ideas generated by the book are valuable for all those concerned with media education.
Marchand, R. (1985) *Advertising the American Dream*, Berkeley: University of California Press.
   A scholarly and attractive book which traces the development of American advertising between 1920 and 1940. There are illustrations of such bizarre advertisements as a flashy girl draped over a coffin, cigarettes are recommended as more healthy than confectionery, and one advertisement shows how a man loses his girl friend because he has not bought a particular brand of garters. Marchand considers whether a study of advertising can offer accurate information about the social values of the period or whether it merely distorts and selects.
Masterman, L. (1980) *Teaching about Television*, London: Macmillan.
   Although the book focuses on secondary education it is essential reading for all would-be media teachers.
Masterman, L. (ed.) (1984) *Television Mythologies: Stars, Shows and Signs*, London: Comedia/MK Media Press.
   A collection of perceptive, analytical essays on popular television.
Masterman, L. (1985) *Teaching the Media*, London: Comedia Publishing Group.
   This book is stimulating and informative for all media teachers. It covers media determinants, rhetoric, ideology and audiences as well as considering the evolution and future of media education. Recommended.
Meyers, W. (1984) *The Image Makers*, London: Macmillan.
   This explains the stories and battles behind the selling of such goods as cola and burgers.
Ministry of Education, Ontario (1989) *Media Literacy: Resource Guide*, Ontario: Ministry of Education.
   After an introduction to media in the curriculum, this handbook offers a wealth of practical suggestions for classroom activities concerning the mass media.

Morley, D. (1986) *Family Television: Cultural Power and Domestic Leisure,* London: Comedia.
A detailed analysis of how eighteen families integrate television into their life styles.

Morsy, Z. (ed.) (1984) *Media Education,* Paris: UNESCO.
Offers a worldwide perspective on trends in media education.

Moss, G. (1989) *Un/Popular Fictions,* London: Virago Press.
Proposes that girls' use of the genre of romantic fiction is not mindless enslavement but rather the readers use the texts to raise questions about social and cultural identities and how these are negotiated.

Murray, J.P. and Salomon, G. (eds) (1984) *The Future of Children's Television,* Nebraska: Boys Town in cooperation with the Markle Foundation.
These are conference papers by eminent American researchers. They are a useful source of references for anyone wishing to look critically at the effects research into how children's television may be an educational resource.

Myers, K. (1986) *Understains . . . The Sense and Seduction of Advertising,* London: Comedia Publishing.
An entertaining, well-illustrated and controversial examination of modern advertising and how the political left needs to use commercial messages.

Noble, G. (1975) *Children in Front of the Small Screen,* London: Constable.
This considers, from a Piagetian perspective, how the child's stage of cognitive development determines how she will interact with, and interpret, what she sees on television.

Packard, V. (1957) *The Hidden Persuaders,* Harmondsworth: Penguin Books.
One of the earliest and most influential studies of advertising techniques of the 1950s. Although it is now dated and perhaps alarmist, it had considerable impact when it was first produced and it is worth reading as a period piece.

Palmer, P. (1986) *The Lively Audience: A Study of Children Around the TV Set,* Sydney: Allen & Unwin.
This scholarly Australian research examines how children interact with television and it challenges the notion that watching television is a passive experience. This interactionist approach makes a nice comparison with the earlier book by Noble which is listed in this bibliography.

Pearson, G. (1983) *Hooligan: A History of Respectable Fears,* London: Macmillan.
A reassuring and carefully documented study which provides evidence that social degeneration is not as rapid as we may be led to believe. Pearson suggests that each generation looks back with rose-coloured glasses and blames the contemporary popular culture for the current evils amongst young people.

Philo, G. (1990) *Seeing and Believing – The Influence of Television*, London: Routledge.
A careful effects study which produces evidence to show that most television viewers believe and retain lasting images of much of what they see on television news broadcasts. The book also contributes to the debate about political bias in the media.

Ploghoft, M. and Anderson, J.A. (1982) *Teaching Critical Viewing Skills: An Integrated Approach*, Illinois: Thomas.
Although this book claims to avoid the effects model – so prevalent in the American literature on the subject of media education – the authors' use of the word 'critical' implies that television's adverse influence needs to be managed. The pedagogy is highly prescriptive but, all this aside, there are some practical ideas which are well worth considering, especially on the subject of advertising.

Pope, D. (1983) *The Making of Modern Advertising*, New York: Basic Books.
This addresses the structural questions behind American advertising up to the 1920s.

Postman, N. and Weingartner, C. (1969) *Teaching as a Subversive Activity*, Harmondsworth: Penguin Education Specials.
In this incisive critique of the imposed curriculum the authors discuss 'What is worth knowing', 'Meaning making' and 'New languages: the media'. This text supports Postman's earlier book *Television and the Teaching of English*, New York: Appleton (1961); however, in *Teaching as a Conserving Activity*, New York: Delacourt (1979), he performs a volte face by writing about his fears that children's learning is damaged by television.

Root, J. (1986) *Open the Box*, London: Comedia Publishing.
Linked to the Channel 4 series of the same name, this positive and non-judgemental book is an easy introductory text for studying television.

Schiller, H. (1981) *Who Knows: Information in the Age of Fortune 500*, New Jersey: Ablex.
Schiller suggests that most people believe that the flow of information from technical sources is free and easily accessible. This he proposes is not the truth but rather in fact information is increasingly becoming a marketable commodity in capitalist terms. He believes that the sooner the truth is revealed the sooner this trend can be challenged.

Schlesinger, P. (1978) *Putting Reality Together*, London: Constable.
A readable study of radio and television broadcasting.

Schudson, M. (1984) *Advertising, the Uneasy Persuasion: Its Dubious Impact on American Society*, New York: Basic Books.
This book contains 'The advertiser's perspective' and 'Advertising as capitalist realism'.

Silverstone, R. (1981) *The Message of Television: Myth and Narrative in Contemporary Culture*, London: Heinemann.
Scholarly and illuminating analyses of the concepts of myth and narrative.

Slater, G. (1987) *Planning the Schedules*, London: Hodder & Stoughton.
A short practical booklet intended for use with secondary pupils but which contains useful ideas for the primary sector.

Smythe, D. (1981) *Dependency Road: Communications, Capitalism, Consciousness and Canada*, New Jersey: Ablex Publishing Corporation.
A disturbing book which argues that audiences are categorised as 'slaves' to be sold to the advertisers. Smythe accuses schools of implicitly imparting submissiveness to authority.

Sontag, S. (1973) *On Photography*, New York: Farrar, Strauss & Giroux.
This series of essays shows how photography confers importance and how the camera can refract reality. The first essay, 'In Plato's cave', is especially worthwhile.

Taylor, L. and Mullan, B. (1986) *Uninvited Guests: The Intimate Secrets of Television and Radio*, London: Coronet Books/Hodder & Stoughton.
Contains extensive transcripts of audience research which enable the reader to gain some insights into various groups of people's responses to television.

Taylor, P. (1985) *The Smoke Ring: Tobacco, Money and Multinational Politics*, London: Sphere Books.
This book shows how the critics of tobacco have been effectively silenced.

Thomson, K. (1987) *Thinking about Images*, London: Hodder & Stoughton.
A short practical text with some useful suggestions, but it seems strange that in a book on image analysis there should be a sexist bias in the booklet's own illustrations.

West Sussex Education Department (1987) *Media Education in Primary Schools*, Sussex: Education Department.
An introductory pamphlet which is useful for those running very short in-service courses.

Williams, R. (1961) *The Long Revolution*, Harmondsworth: Penguin Books in association with Chatto & Windus.
Contains a discussion of the theory of culture and a study of such social institutions as education and the press.

Williams, R. (1974) *Television: Technology and Cultural Form*, London: Fontana/Collins.
This book raises the important issue of how television, as a technological cultural form, needs to be considered in terms not of separate programmes but rather of the way it flows.

Williams, R. (1976) *Keywords*, London: Flamingo/Fontana.
A fascinating 'dictionary' showing how language has evolved and reflects our culture and society.

Williamson, J. (1978) *Decoding Advertisements*, London: Marion Boyars Publishers.
A well-illustrated, if somewhat dated, detailed analysis of the ideology of advertising.

Winick, M.P. and Winick, C. (1979) *The Television Experience: What Children See*, Beverly Hills: Sage Publications.
A careful examination of the differences between the ways in which various age groups of children respond to television.

JOURNALS

The journals *Screen* and *Screen Education* (now combined), *Journal of Educational Television* and *Journal of Communication* all provide invaluable reading for the media teacher.

Index